THE THEORY OF
COLLECTIVE BARGAINING

THE THEORY OF
COLLECTIVE
BARGAINING

A HISTORY, ANALYSIS AND CRITICISM
OF THE PRINCIPAL THEORIES WHICH
HAVE SOUGHT TO EXPLAIN THE
EFFECTS OF TRADE UNIONS AND
EMPLOYERS' ASSOCIATIONS UPON THE
DISTRIBUTION OF THE PRODUCT OF
INDUSTRY

By W. H. Hutt

WITH A PREFACE BY LUDWIG VON MISES

THE FREE PRESS, GLENCOE, ILLINOIS

ERRATA

Page 17: Line 8—should read "affected" instead of "effected"

Page 29: First line of footnote—should be "of" instead of "on"

Page 30: Line 2—"no matter" was omitted after "in form"

Page 68: Line 15—"that it means anything more than" was repeated

Page 93: Line 11—should read "is" instead of "in"

Page 93: Line 19—the last "i" was omitted from the word "principle"

Page 123: Line 7—the word "overhead" was omitted after the word "heavy"

Page 126: Lines 11 & 12—"a large falling off in numbers employed it may have prevented" repeated

Page 141: Last line—there should be no "s" on "opinion"

INDEX

Errors, which appeared in the original text and have not been corrected in this printing, are found on the following pages:

Page 24: Line 2—should be "absurdities" instead of "adsurdities"

Page 55: Line 18—the word "the" omitted before the word "last"

Page 104: Line 9—the period was omitted after "altogether"

Page 144: Line 19—the word "dyke" misspelled—should be "dike"

To
ARNOLD AND EDITH PLANT

Contents

Preface to the
New American Edition

ECONOMICS TEACHES that there is but one method available to raise wage rates for all those eager to earn wages, viz., to increase the per-head quota of capital invested and thereby the marginal productivity of labor.

At the wage rate established on a free labor market all those who are eager to hire workers can hire as many as they want and all those who want to earn wages can find a job. On a free labor market there prevails a tendency to make unemployment disappear. Not to interfere with the operation of the labor market is the only effective full-employment policy.

If either by government decree or by union pressure and compulsion wage rates are raised above the potential market rate, unemployment of a part of the potential labor force becomes a lasting phenomenon. It is impossible for the unions to raise wage rates for all those eager to earn wages and to find jobs. If they win for some groups of workers higher compensation than what they would have collected on an unhampered market, they victimize other groups.

It took much more than a century to attain this cognition. Quite understandably people sympathize with the impatience of wage earners who want to find a more rapid means for the improvement of their material conditions than that provided by the progressive accumulation of capital. The economists were not to blame for the fact that emotionally they agreed in this regard with the majority. What was wrong with the attitude of many of the older economists was that they blithely endorsed popular fallacies about the methods to be applied for the realization of this desirable end. One of the foremost social functions of economics is to explode current misconceptions about the fitness of means to attain definite ends chosen. The classical economists and their followers did a marvellous job in exposing prevailing errors concerning foreign trade, government tutelage of business, money, credit and so on. But they not only left the union doctrine intact, they even tried to find a justification for it. It was a hopeless task, and it entangled its authors in a maze of contradictions and inconsistencies. However, we must be grateful to them for the pains they bestowed upon the problems. For it was precisely the failure of their scrupulous exertions that made it easier for later generations to arrive at a more correct solution of the problems involved.

Professor Hutt's brilliant essay is not merely a contribution to the history of economic thought. It is rather a critical analysis of the arguments advanced by economists from Adam Smith down and by the spokesmen of the unions in favor of the thesis that unionism can raise wage rates above the market level without harm to anybody else than the "exploiters." As such it is of utmost use not only to every student of economics but to everybody who wants to form a well-founded opinion about one of the most vital as well as most controversial political issues of our age.

LUDWIG VON MISES

New York, March, 1954

Author's Preface

PART OF THIS ESSAY was included in papers read to the Economic Society of South Africa at Cape Town on the 18th September, 1928, and to Section "F" of the British Association at Johannesburg on the 2nd August, 1929. The study on which it is based arose out of doubts as to the validity of much current teaching on the subject which had been suggested in the lectures of Professor Edwin Cannan. My indebtedness to his teaching and methods must be obvious. I must also acknowledge the help, direct and indirect, that I have received from the criticism and encouragement of Professor Arnold Plant.

I have no prefatorial apologies to make. The essay is brief, but brevity I claim as a virtue. It is absolutely untopical, but in avoiding reference to current events or controversy I may lessen suspicion of partisanship. In content and exposition it will have many defects, but I have attempted a difficult task which others have neglected. It is strange that

there should be a complete absence of any modern
treatise on the theory of trade unionism, for there
is a colossal literature on its organization and history. We have, it is true, the Webbs' *Industrial
Democracy*, but that famous work is respected as
a study of the government and organization of unionism rather than as a contribution to economic theory.
My attempt may help to fill the gap until it is superseded by a better one.

The need was expressed by the Secretary of the
General Federation of Trade Unions, Mr. W. A.
Appleton, in his book *Trade Unions, their Past,
Present, and Future*, 1925. He said (pp. 136-7):

"To ensure the consideration of trade unionism as a
fundamental industrial problem, and apart from inherited
or acquired prejudices and unbiassed by its possible appli-
cations, requires the type of mind which is sometimes
developed in the universities, but which is seldom found
in the partisan atmosphere of the actual movement. Few
men in the movement realise its complexities or the need
for abstract study as a preparation for official work, and
fewer still there are who, apprehending, possess the time,
the temperament and the capacity for the task. It is
rather in the world of economics and letters that one may
hope to find men who have not only the temperamental
aptitudes and scientific attainments required for a study
of the movement, but also the leisure which financial
competence gives. It may indeed be groups of men en-

gaged in research, deduction and explanation who will elucidate the philosophy of trade unionism and tell us what ought to be, and what can be."

Now, I cannot claim to possess the qualities of Mr. Appleton's ideal student and, unfortunately, I do not think he would endorse my conclusions. Yet, on the above quotation, I base my defense against those "practical men" who would decry these pages as the work of an academic theorist; and from it also I gather hope that some trade-union officials at least may endeavor to understand the thoughts of a detached and independent student of the institution they control.

I hardly dare express a hope that existing legislators will condescend to read what I have written. The student has to face the fact that many men of action find continuous intellectual effort irksome; he must cheerfully recognize that practically none of those people appointed to make laws controlling wages, or to make actual wage-board determinations, have even the most elementary understanding of issues such as those discussed here. The hope that rational thought may one day be imported as an active force into this field of human activity lies mainly in the universities. The student of today may, in some few cases, be the legislator of tomorrow, and he may carry with him and transmit some glimmering of enlightenment.

It is, thus, to the genuine student (in whatever class of society he may happen to be) rather than to the practical man that this book is addressed. Adult school tutors and W.E.A. tutors should find it of assistance even if they are unable to accept its conclusions. Those who have made no systematic study of economic theory will be unable to understand the compressed argument which follows, but it should not be too difficult for any perservering student who has mastered, say, the Ruskin College correspondence course in economics or who is thoroughly familiar with any good elementary book on economics. The subject is a difficult one and I am afraid that my discussion will be read with ease only by the fairly advanced student. A satisfactory "popular" work is beyond my powers and, perhaps, impossible. The student who is not familiar with the Webbs' *Industrial Democracy* should read Part II, Chapters XII and XIII; and Part III, Chapters I and II of that work before tackling my contribution.

The popularity of economics has happily greatly extended in recent decades. But the study of wage questions has, it seems to me, been handicapped all along by the vague and erroneous ideas which I endeavor here to sweep away. So long as it was held that there was an increment of real income which could be transferred from the relatively rich to the relatively poor by control of wage rates, it was essential that a satisfactory wage theory should show exactly what that increment was and how control effected the transfer. Instead of this we were given phrases about combination leading to "equality of bargaining power" and wage fixation protecting "the economically weak." Critics have often complained in recent years of the lack of a realistic theory of wages. The purging of the discussion of these misleading ideas and phrases may, perhaps, clear the way for more useful investigations into the working of the value mechanism in the sphere of labor's remuneration.

W. H. HUTT.

University of Cape Town, March, 1930.

PART ONE

"Labor's Disadvantage"

THE OBJECT of this essay is to controvert the suggestions typical of most modern economic text-books, (*a*) that there is some portion of the normal remuneration of labor which, in the absence of collective bargaining by labor is, or can be, transferred to the remuneration of other factors of production owing to labor's "disadvantage in bargaining"; or (*b*) that combination, by increasing labor's "bargaining power," enables it to acquire a part of the normal remuneration of some other factor.

THE TERM
"COLLECTIVE BARGAINING"

The very useful term "Collective Bargaining" was coined in 1891 by Mrs. Sidney Webb in her work on the cooperative movement. The Webbs[1] have

---

1. This is the only sensible way of referring to Lord Passfield and Mrs. Webb. No disrespect is intended. It is the penalty of their greatness.

never given a formal definition but have used it to cover negotiations between employers and workpeople when the workpeople act in concert and the employer meets "a collective will." Collective bargaining may take place in many kinds of negotiating in concert, but it is used here to describe what is probably the most important function of trade unionism.

THE SUPPOSED IMPORTANCE OF THE ABANDONMENT OF THE WAGE-FUND THEORY

It is commonly believed that the overthrow of the "Wage-Fund" theory was the turning-point in regard to the economist's attitude towards trade unionism. The earlier economists, we are told, held that the level of wages depended on the proportion of the wage-fund or capital in relation to the number of workers. Trade unions could not affect the size of this fund and hence all efforts to raise the general level of wages were futile. Gains by one section of the workers could only be obtained at the expense of other sections. With the abandonment of the wage-fund error, however, and especially after Mill's renunciation of it in 1869, this view was shown to be untenable, so we are told, and from that time the economic justification of trade unions has been complete. Professor Clay, for instance, tells us that the wage-fund theory was responsible for the belief, common in the middle class, that political economy had found trade unionism to be futile because of the theory that "if wages were fixed by the proportion between population and capital, trade unionism was futile and wicked; it could raise the wages of one section only at the expense of other sections."[2] Successive reiterations by leading economists have caused this belief to become firmly accepted. F. A. Walker, in 1876, declared that under the wage-fund doctrine the striking workman was regarded as "an irrational animal whose instincts, unfortunately, were not politico-economical."[3] Edgeworth, writing in 1881, declared that "in the matter of trade unionism . . . the untutored mind of the workman had gone more straight to the point than economic intelligence misled by a bad method."[4] Cunningham, in 1892 said: "Men were continually regretting the blind stupidity of working men who thought that combinations could raise wages . . . but this was a blunder. Combinations can raise wages; they have done so and may do so again."[5] This belief in a fundamental change having been effected by the

---

2. *Economics for the General Reader*, p. 313.
3. *The Wages Question*, p. 144.
4. *Mathematical Psychics*, p. 45.
5. *Economic Journal*, 1892, p. 14.

giving up of the clumsy wage-fund theory is erroneous and misleading. The realization of the absurdities of the doctrine gave the apologists of the unions something they could attack with the full support of authority; but the productivity theory which, in various forms, arose on its ruins did not in itself contain any justification for collective bargaining. The vague phrases about the "disadvantage" of uncombined labor which constitute its modern defense have existed continuously since the days of Adam Smith.

ATTEMPTS TO RATIONALIZE IDEAS ABOUT "LABOR'S DISADVANTAGE"

The change of doctrine that was supposed to have taken place in the 'seventies was heralded by four mainly independent[6] but remarkably similar defenses of workers' combinations. The authors were: F. D. Longe, Cliffe Leslie, Fleeming Jenkin and W. T. Thornton. Three of them definitely attacked the wage-fund conception, but the principal object of all four, although Longe denied it, was the justification of unionism. These contributions all appeared during the years 1866 to 1869, and were followed in 1869 by an article from Mill (in the *Fortnightly Review*), who, it seems, had only read the views of

---

6. Leslie *had* read Longe, some articles by Thornton and Jenkin, and Jacob Waley's paper (referred to later).

his friend Thornton. It was in this article that he formally renounced the wage-fund theory and gave *currency* to the view that there was some way in which trade unions could gain, not at the expense of other workers but at the expense of the capitalist. An attempt to analyze separately and carefully every single theory put forward by all these writers has led to the conclusion that they consist largely in the rationalization of ideas about labor's disadvantage in bargaining which, far from being novel, had been held continuously since the time of Adam Smith. For the rest they seem at first to contain little beyond a number of attacks on the general theory of prices based on generalizations induced from the consideration of a number of hypothetical and improbable special cases, and a number of newly coined descriptive phrases which have since served as a substitute for thought in these matters.

THE IDEA OF "LABOR'S DISADVANTAGE" ACCEPTED BY WAGE-FUND THEORISTS

Adam Smith, who was the first to talk about "the funds destined for the payment of labour," held views about the laborer's disadvantage which were not unlike those of Marshall. M'Culloch had a typical defense of workers' combinations. It is only when workers act, he said, "in that simultaneous manner which is equivalent to a combination . . . that it becomes the immediate interest of the masters to comply with their demand." (Without) "an open or avowed, or (of) a tacit and real combination, workmen would not be able to obtain a rise of wages by their own exertion, but would be left to depend on the competition of their masters."[7] Even Fawcett, the wage-fund die-hard who, for many years after Mill, his master, had given up the theory still clung affectionately to it, held quite the usual sort of views justifying collective bargaining. "I believe it can be easily shown," he wrote, "that the labourer is placed at a disadvantage, if he attempts simply as an individual to arrange this bargain, and I further believe that labourers must show that they have the power of combining, in order at all times to be able to sell their labour on the best possible terms."[8] The ultimate defense of unionism in Mill's 1869 article—the bold justification of monopoly—differed in no respect from the justification which he put forward in his *Principles* while he still believed in the wage-fund. Those excluded did not suffer for their wages would, in any case, have been kept down to subsistence level. "Combinations to keep up wages," he wrote, "are

---

7. *Treatise on Wages*, p. 79.
8. *Economic Position of the British Labourer*, 1865, p. 173.

therefore not only permissible, but useful, whenever really calculated to have that effect."[9] On the other hand, the chief critic of the supposed new tendencies, T. S. Cree, in an essay praised but not heeded by Marshall, declared that "the correctness of the wages fund is not at all necessary for my position."[10] Curiously enough, the two authorities whose condemnation of unionism was almost unconditional objected also to the wage-fund conception. Mountifort Longfield's *Lectures on Political Economy*, 1834, is notable chiefly for its anticipation of the productivity theory; yet its object was, to use his own words, "to show how impossible it is to regulate wages generally either by combinations of workmen, or by legislative enactments." And Hermann in Germany blamed the wage-fund error for encouraging unionism and causing strikes "by its doctrine that the source of wages is the capital of the 'entrepreneur.' . . ."[11] These facts seem to have been overlooked by the Webbs or else regarded by them as of no importance at all. For, in seventeen references to M'Culloch and three to Fawcett in their *Industrial Democracy*, they make no mention of the grounds on which these economists

---

9. *Principles*, Chap. X.
10. *Criticism of the Theory of Trade Unionism*, 1891, p. 24.
11. Quoted by Crook, *German Wage Theories*, p. 28.

sought to justify unionism; and they are two of the three authorities quoted in a footnote (on page 606) to support the contention that belief in the wage-fund theory as enunciated by them was the reason why public opinion "unhesitatingly refuted Trade Unionism."[12] In twenty-five references to Mill they do not quote the grounds on which he approved of their monopolistic policy. Neither do they notice the arguments of Mountifort Longfield, whose name appears in a footnote. And they quote a passage suggesting the wage-fund formula from Cree, but do not mention his claim that the theory was irrelevant to his criticisms. Articulate trade-union leaders accepted readily the wage-fund formula. At least two sets of trade-union rules actually quoted M'Culloch,[13] thousands of whose pamphlets circulated among and were approved of by working-class leaders of his day.[14] An essay which declared the orthodox political economy of the 'fifties to be undisputed[15] was

---

12. In an earlier draft of part of this essay, circulated to a number of friends, I wrongly included C. Morrison as a wage-fund economist accepting the doctrine of "labor's disadvantage." —W. H. H.

13. E.g. "Articles of the West Riding Fancy Union. . . . 1824." Quoted in *Report of the Select Committee on the Combination Laws*, 1825, p. 27. Cf. a *London Trades Committee* report in 1838 (p. 5), in the Place Add. MSS. 27835:104.

14. E.g. See Place Add. MSS. 27803:294, 347, 478, 516.

15. T. J. Dunning, *Trade Unions and Strikes*, 1859, pp. 4-5.

passed by a large union as a faithful representation of their views.[16] Even the supposed enemies of unions had often absorbed the typical belief in their beneficence. Sheriff Alison, detested by the unions for his stern suppression of the disorders of the famous Glasgow cotton spinners' strike of 1838, gave evidence (before the Parliamentary Enquiry on Combinations, 1838)[17] to the effect that workmen's combinations enabled the "members to a certain degree to compensate and to enter with equality into the lists with capital," and by 1860, as Sir Archibald Alison, his views had not changed. "Without combinations," he said, "competition would force wages down and workers would be reduced to the condition of serfs in Russia or the Ryots of Hindostan."[18]

THE THEORY OF COLLECTIVE BARGAINING A MERE ATTACHMENT TO WHATEVER PARTICULAR WAGE THEORY HAS BEEN HELD

The truth is, that the theory explaining or showing the desirability of collective bargaining has always been quite independent of the wages doctrine

---

16. A recent writer puts the date on the change in the attitude of unionism in the 'nineties. Hitherto, ". . . it had taken for granted the current doctrines of 'the wages fund,' 'the law of supply and demand' and so forth." (Rayner, *The Story of Trade Unionism*, p. 63).

17. Q. 1956.

18. *Rep. of the Nat. Assn. for the Prom. of Social Science*, 1860.

that has existed at any time; it has been very similar in form to what particular theory it has been attached; but it has always been a kind of attachment to the theory and not, as we should expect, in view of unionism being the most obvious institution forming part of the wage-determining mechanism, an integral part of it. This fact alone would suggest that nothing very important or fundamental is involved in such a theory. A few economists have ignored it altogether in a way which would suggest that they regard it as empty although they have not directly attacked it.[19] For example, Professor Cannan writes: "Modern doctrine teaches plainly enough that combinations of earners can only raise earnings if they can raise the value or quantity of the product . . ."[20] This clearly cuts out any theory of collective bargaining, for that is concerned with the *distribution* and not the *size* or *value* of the product. He adds that in practice it is shown by common observation and careful investigation that little can be done by combinations of earners unless they have power to prevent outsiders from entering the trade.[21] All that is admitted here is that individual groups may gain

19. The recent publication of Cannan's *Review of Economic Theory* provides an exception to this statement.
20. *Theories of Production and Distribution*, Third Edn., p. 404.
21. *Op. cit.*, p. 404.

at the expense of others by monopoly obtained by the device of exclusion; and that was what the earlier economists appeared, at times, to say. But *does* direct exclusion supply a sufficient explanation of the effect of combinations on wages? It is desirable briefly to examine this view before discussing the theories which appear to contradict it.

THE INTERESTS OF THE UNIONISTS ARE ANTAGONISTIC TO THOSE OF THE LABORING MASSES

Frederic Harrison described the trade-union movement as "one universal protest against injustice from the whole field of labour." This identification with the general working-class movement (although very common) may be highly misleading. It probably arose from the fact that typical ignorant upper-class opinion during the nineteenth century was quite unable to appreciate the complexity of the social and economic tendencies operating among the "lower orders." To them, there was only one working class—an inferior class that, led by demagogues and agitators, was trying to usurp political and economic power. Apart from the economists, a few enlightened industrialists and a few philosophers, they had a vague belief that the drudgery of the masses was necessary for the leisure of the few, that their subservience was the natural order of things, and that low wages were good for trade. They were very glad to have it on the authority of the economists that these evil and rebellious combinations were ineffectual. But this should not allow the modern student to ignore the fact that the interests of the unionists were almost universally antagonistic to those of the laboring masses. Had historians of the trade-union movement been orthodox economic theorists they might have laid the strongest emphasis on this point. As it happens, however, they have been practically without exception persons with an undisguised hostility to orthodox theory; and this may account for their failure to stress what might have struck other economists most forcibly. The Webbs frankly admit the frequent existence of monopolistic tendencies on the part of unions, but the general impression they leave is misleading for they have obviously written as union advocates. However much we may admire their *History*—a monumental achievement which it would be presumptuous to praise—we must remind ourselves, whilst we are influenced by its thoroughness and manifest sincerity, that it is yet the special pleading of those who have devoted their lives to the encouragement of the institution whose development they were recording.

OPINIONS OF WORKING-CLASS LEADERS

To justify the contention that combinations were antagonistic to the interests of the great majority of the laboring classes is impossible by means of ordinary historical method in a mainly theoretical treatment such as this. We can, however, to escape the suspicion of bias or misrepresentation, appeal to the opinions, expressed at different times, of working-class leaders themselves. This is not the most satisfactory way of indicating the position, but it is the most practicable one in the present case.

THE "FOUNDER OF SCIENTIFIC SOCIALISM"

We might appeal first to William Thompson. Described by Menger as "the most eminent founder of modern scientific Socialism," the originator of the idea of "surplus value,"[22] a friend and teacher of Robert Owen, Thompson can hardly be regarded as a biased witness against working-class bodies. He was, we are told, of the most kindly and gentle disposition, but when he considered the workmen's combinations of his day he was moved to passionate condemnation of them. To him they were "bloody aristocracies of industry." "The apprenticeship or excluding system,"

22. According to Menger. It has been disputed by Dr. Bonar among others.

he said, "depended on mere force and would not allow other workers to come into the market at any price." "It matters not," he said in 1827, "whether that force . . . be the gift of law or whether it be assumed by the tradesmen in spite of the law: it is equally mere force."[23] They demonstrated to him "the inefficiency of force supported regulations, though backed with political power, to keep up generally throughout the country the remuneration of any species of labour; though they certainly have tended . . . to keep up the remuneration of the few within the circle of the combination." Such gains were always "at the expense of the equal right of the industrious to acquire skill and to exchange their labour where and how they may."[24] This is "the founder of scientific Socialism" speaking—not an employer. "Will they then resort to force," he said, "law supported as to apprenticeships or illegal as to intimidation—in all cases equally hateful—to put down the competition of the great majority of the industrious and thus erect a bloody—for force will lead to blood and without blood no aristocracy can be supported—aristocracy of industry?"[25]

---

23. *Labour Rewarded*, 1827, p. 75.
24. *Ibid.*, pp. 76-77.
25. *Ibid.*, p. 81.

A SOUTH AFRICAN PARALLEL

The position which raised the ire of Thompson a century ago finds a close and obvious parallel in South Africa today. If he had been writing at the present day, and the South African trade unions had condescended to reply, they would probably have answered: "Those whom we exclude are, on the whole, 'non-Europeans,' a morally inferior class to whom we do no harm by our exclusive policy as, owing to their low standard of life, they cannot rise and can merely drag us down." Curiously enough this was just the view of the English unions of last century towards the "knobsticks" or "scabs," the great majority of the laboring classes who were outside the unions. Their typical attitude was well summarized by J. S. Mill in his attempted justification of enlightened unionism in 1869. *Acting as the unions' advocate* he put the following words into the mouth of their witness: "Those whom we exclude are a morally inferior class of labourers to us; their labour is worthless and their want of prudence and self-restraint makes them more active in adding to the population. We do them no wrong by intrenching ourselves behind a barrier, to exclude those whose competition would bring down our wages, without more than momentarily raising theirs, but only adding to the total numbers in existence."[26] *Apart from the Malthusian aspect,* this argument seems to be a fair representation of trade-union opinion at the time Mill wrote.

THE APATHY OF DEPRESSED CLASSES

One may wonder why it was that the working classes in England did not protest more at such injustices. To some extent it may have been for the same reason that we get so few protests against unions from "non-Europeans" in South Africa. It often appeared as if the "knobstick" felt and believed himself to be an inferior person. Another friend and defender of the trade-union movement, writing a year before Mill in the passage just quoted, described the knobstick's position thus: "The wretched knobstick . . . is jeered at and snubbed on all possible occasions . . . he receives none of those little aids by which the other men lighten one another's labour . . . he is generally an inferior workman, and his work receives its full due of criticism; he is an outcast, a pariah, and fear of personal violence is not required to render this position a wretched one. Some societies will not allow him to work in the same shop with their members, even as though he tainted the air. . . .

---

26. *Fortnightly Review,* 1869.

Odd as it may seem, the knobstick takes much the same view of his position; he feels himself a sneak. . . . He is unskilful, poor, weak and a traitor (for attempting to undercut); they are skilled, rich, strong and noble; yes, even when they morally kick him. . . ."[27]

PROTESTS AGAINST EXCLUSIVENESS

Mill's attempts to justify exclusiveness did not pass without criticism. "After all," said Dr. Stirling, "the knobstick is not an outlaw, to be cut off from personal freedom and the protection of the law. He has his rights like his betters; and though too often treated like the leper of old, his chief offence is, after all, his poverty."[28] And T. S. Cree, referring to the Malthusian backing to Mill's argument, remarked that Malthus "never proposed the destruction of the weak by the strong, in order that the latter should have more to divide."[29]

UNIONIST APATHY TO CHARTISM

Until they obtained political power the great mass of the laboring classes had few friends outside their

27. Fleeming Jenkin, "Trade Unions," in *North British Review,* 1868. Reprinted in his *Collected Papers.* Compare Webb, *History,* p. 296.

28. Stirling, "Mr. Mill on Trades Unions" in *Recess Studies,* 1870, p. 330.

29. Cree, *op. cit.,* p. 28.

own ranks. Apart from the fact that there were no classes below them whom they could exploit by exclusion, they could not afford the luxury of unions or any other societies; nor could they pay leaders. Organizations of laborers offered no careers to competent organizers until well on into the century when the course of economic progress had greatly increased their resources. Thus we find that the Chartist Movement, the most prominent genuine working-class movement of the earlier half of the century, received little support from the unions. Their apathy brought fierce denunciation from Feargus O'Connor. "Never," he wrote, "was there more criminal apathy." The denunciations of Daniel O'Connell went much deeper. He condemned in the severest language not only the existing practices of the Irish Unions but also the essential exclusiveness of all attempts at the regulation of wages by combination.[30] The reply of the London Trades Combination Committee to O'Connell was hardly repentant.[31]

IN MORE RECENT TIMES THE OLD ANTAGONISMS STILL OCCASIONALLY APPARENT

When at length, owing to the growth in the economic and political power of the masses, unionism

---

30. Cf. Ryan, *The Irish Labour Movement*, pp. 89, 90.
31. *Combinations Defended*, 1839, p. 42.

began to extend its ranks the hostility to the older interests was obvious. John Burns, in the 'eighties, was contemptuous of existing unions. "Mere middle and upper class rate reducing institutions," he called them. The "Dockers' Strike" which he organized heralded a new era which brought into trade unions workers in unskilled occupations. This led to a rapid expansion during the late 'nineties and the early part of this century, during which period the earlier tendency to hostility tended, for many reasons, to die down. Not that the opposition of interest had gone. In the 'nineties exclusiveness still had its unashamed apostles. Miss Clementina Black admitted that no doubt trade unions did "tend to make the battle of life harder for the incompetent and shiftless." They tend, she said, "to make a boundary line on the one side of which is the well-paid man in work and the other side the absolutely unpaid man out of work." But this, she argued, brought no real injury to the community.[32]

THE "NEW UNIONISM" OBSCURED BUT DID NOT DESTROY THE OLD OPPOSITION OF INTEREST BETWEEN ONE CLASS OF WORKERS AND ANOTHER

Nevertheless, as the proportion of organized workers grew the real antagonism between those with

32. *Contemporary Review*, 1892.

effective exclusive power and those without became more and more obscured. Some regarded the "New Unionism" as a movement which completely superseded the old and exclusive system. " 'The Masses' have been as ready to group themselves in exclusive sections, according to income, as their 'betters,' " said H. H. Champion in 1890, "and the greatest sinners in this respect have been the Trades Unionists. But of late a different feeling has arisen. . . ."[33] Whether exclusive power or desire was checked in the 'nineties is doubtful: but it was certainly not becoming more noticeable. Occasionally, however, we still found an over-earnest or disgruntled leader refusing to deny the existence of the old antagonisms. "The exclusiveness of some of the existing unions," said Tom Mann in 1911, "must be got rid of . . . the skilled men must throw off that silly notion of superiority. . . . That unionism whose object is to maintain a special preserve for the privileged few must disappear, for it is incompatible with the rights of workmen generally and is a menace to industrial solidarity." In America we see the same thing. From the I.W.W. we occasionally get the same kind of protests against exclusiveness. And the French "syndi-

---

33. *The Great Dock Strike*, 1890.

calists" have expressed themselves in almost the same words.

EXCLUDED CLASSES STILL APATHETIC

But from the classes who, in modern society, suffer most from union exclusiveness we get the fewest protests. They accept quietly and unquestioningly their traditional economic inferiority. When the "colored" or "native" workers in South Africa organize, or when women organize in countries which are racially homogeneous, we either find them establishing new exclusions or else adopting the principle of "equal pay for equal work"—thus renouncing the only means in their power of discounting the prejudice against them as a class. Of course, organization of such workers is sometimes necessary in order to get or preserve the effective or even the *legal* right to a trade.

THE "STANDARD RATE" ESSENTIALLY AN EXCLUDING DEVICE

The exclusive policy of unions is not confined to the obvious method of visible exclusion by apprenticeship restrictions and the like. Every insistence on an artificially high rate will tend to reduce the number it will be profitable to employ. Those within the combination will still benefit at the expense of those outside. This method of obtaining monopoly is more pernicious than that of apprenticeship exclusion as it enables the monopolists to plead that they are acting in the interests of those whom they are in fact excluding. They can claim that they are raising the standard of living of the very ones whose competition they wish to eliminate, and even get the support of legal enactment to enable them to carry out their policy. The evil in labor monopolies lies not only in their driving the less fortunate to relatively badly paid occupations but also in their raising the cost of living to them as well.

THE WAGE-FUND THEORY ITSELF DID NOT JUSTIFY THE POPULAR BELIEF OF THE TIME THAT POLITICAL ECONOMY CONDEMNED ALL STRIKES AS IRRATIONAL

In view of the obviously purely monopolistic nature of workmen's combinations in their day, there is nothing surprising in the classical economists' failure to give much attention to the question as to whether or not the members of a union could increase their incomes otherwise than at the expense of other workers. *An elaborate theory of collective bargaining would not have been much more than the merest academic abstraction in their day.* Where they can be blamed is in not having faced more boldly this question of exclusiveness. It is true that on the whole they condemned it, but they seemed rather reluctant to admit its power. They often appear to have been trying to leave the impression that all strikes must necessarily fail in the long run and that no group of workers could gain permanently by strike action. This sort of thing was very comforting to the employers and the Press, and until the 'seventies it was made use of in the most careless manner. The economists were said to have declared that combinations could not raise wages. If they were right the workers were fools. But surely what the economists (apart from their sophism about labor's disadvantage) had been saying or trying to say was that unions could not raise wages in general: it had never been explicitly denied that those particular groups could, by combination, increase their own share of the wage-fund at the expense of others, although it was sometimes argued that such monopolies were bound to break down in the end through the competition of other workers (generally from abroad), or through capital being driven elsewhere. The inadequacy of the wage-fund conception allowed this careless thinking to persist—comforting employers yet having no effect in preventing strikes. But modern theories would credit unions with some power of benefiting their members without the exercise of exclusiveness. Let us examine how the various ideas contained in these modern theories came to be held.

THE IDEA OF "LABOR'S DISADVANTAGE" IS FOUND IN "THE WEALTH OF NATIONS"

The distinctive ideas that lie behind still-persisting theories which seek, without defending monopoly, to justify collective bargaining, originated, as has already been pointed out, with Adam Smith. They arose in connection with the subsistence theory he put forward. Mr. C. M. Lloyd, a leading advocate and historian of unionism, either does not realize this or is very ungrateful for it. "The influence of manufacturers," he writes, ". . . bore heavily upon Parliament . . . in 1776, this influence was reinforced by Adam Smith's *Wealth of Nations*, from which it appeared that the creed of unrestricted exploitation was really a new gospel for humanity."[34] This is a strange way of referring to one of whom it has been said: "(his) sympathies, indeed, seem to have been wholly with the industrious wage-earner, and especially with the poorest."[35] To suggest that Adam Smith favored low wages is entirely false. The suggestion is constantly reiterated that the classical econo-

---

34. C. M. Lloyd, *Trade Unionism*, p. 4.
35. Cannan, *Economist's Protests*, p. 422.

mists generally "defended subsistence wages." "Of all the libels upon them invented by socialist and semi-socialist writers," says Professor Cannan, "this is about the worst. They may have been, they certainly were, wrong about the causes of high wages, but they were always in favour of them."[36] The real evil in the subsistence theory lay in its hopelessness, and the attitude of self-pity and dependence which it tended, right against the spirit of the age, to instil in the minds of the laboring classes. Harriett Martineau, whose views are so often misrepresented as harsh, was attacked by the *Edinburgh Review* for her sentimentalism. They wrote: "From a wish, we suppose, to address the men in conciliatory language, she condoles with them as a suffering race who were induced to strike by the depression of their wages to the lowest point."

ADAM SMITH LIMITED HIS THEORY (WHICH CONTAINED THREE IDEAS) TO "ORDINARY OCCASIONS"

Adam Smith's views bearing on what became later the theory of collective bargaining arose then out of the subsistence theory. "Upon all ordinary occasions," he wrote, "the masters have the advantage in the dispute," and can force the men "into a com-

---

36. *Ibid.*, p. 423.

pliance with their terms." His explanation of this vague power can be analyzed into three separate ideas. First, there existed particular combinations of masters who agreed to force down wages to subsistence level. Second, there was "a tacit but uniform combination" among employers to keep wages down. Third, that although in the long run the workmen might be "as necessary to his master as his master is to him," the necessity is "not so immediate." Whereas masters, "though they did not employ a single workman, could generally live a year or two upon the stocks which they have already acquired," many workmen "could not subsist a week, few could subsist a month, and scarce any a year without employment."[37] These factors, he thought, accounted for the employers' power to force wages down to the subsistence level. He seems to have assumed that *how* they gave the employers this remarkable power was self-evident, for no further explanation of them was given. The emptiness of the theory becomes clear when we consider the limits he assigned to the employers' power in this respect. The limits were determined, not by the individual's minimum requirements for survival, but by those of his family, because otherwise, said Smith, "it would be impossible for

---

37. *Wealth of Nations*, Book I, Chap. VIII.

him to bring up a family, and the race of workmen could not last beyond the first generation." But as Professor Cannan asks, if the masters have this power why should they concern themselves about the labor supply of the next generation? "Trade rings," he says, "usually adopt the motto, 'After us the deluge.'" and he points out that Adam Smith himself probably thought the doctrine was weak as evidenced by his dragging in an irrelevant reference to such wages being the lowest "consistent with common humanity."[38] Moreover, observing that in practice wages were often considerably higher than subsistence level, Smith limited the application of his theory to "ordinary occasions."

ADAM SMITH HIMSELF SEEMS TO HAVE UNCONSCIOUSLY GIVEN UP THE IDEA

Do the *exceptional* occasions help us to understand the theory? He mentioned only one exceptional occasion, and that was an "increase of revenue or stock" which would "sometimes give the labourers an advantage, and enable them to raise their wages." They could do this because the masters would then "bid against one another in order to get workmen, and thus voluntarily break through the natural combina-

---

38. See Cannan, *Theories . . . , op. cit.*, p. 235.

tion of masters not to raise wages." This, he thought, would happen while expansion was in progress. Thus we arrive at the really remarkable conclusion that an increase of stock *loses* the masters their relative advantage, a conclusion which could be made to look like a direct contradiction to the previous contention that it was the greater stocks held by the master which gave him his advantage. The truth is that Adam Smith had really unconsciously given up his earlier theory. In Professor Cannan's words: "The power of the masters to depress wages to the sub-sistence level by combination, and their 'common humanity' which prevents them killing the goose that laid the golden eggs, by depressing them below that level, both disappear. . . . So little room is left for the subsistence theory that Adam Smith seems, to-wards the end of his work, to have forgotten that he had ever held it."[39] But the ideas about the em-ployer's advantage and his power to force down wages indefinitely and the workman's corresponding disadvantage which originated thus have persisted right through to the present day, although the basis on which Adam Smith himself had founded them had been tacitly renounced.

------

39. *Ibid.*, p. 237.

MASTERS' COMBINATIONS FOR DEALING WITH WAGES SEEM
TO HAVE BEEN RELUCTANT AND RETALIATORY UNTIL LATE
IN THE NINETEENTH CENTURY

We shall now proceed to examine the history and development of the three ideas that were connected with his statement of the subsistence theory. We shall deal first with the allegation that masters habitually formed themselves into combinations to force wages down. (The *power* of masters' combinations to force down wages will be discussed at a later stage.) Some informal combinations of masters undoubtedly occasionally got together in his day; and there is no reason for believing that these combinations were anything new. More's *Utopia* talks about a "conspiracy of rich men," discussing "how to hire and abuse the work and labour of the poor for as little money as may be." This kind of idea probably recurred from time to time right up to the time of Adam Smith. Nevertheless, his contention is misleading. Workmen's combinations equally existed in his day, and it is a question of some importance whether masters' combinations led to the formation of unions or whether it worked the other way. A recent article by Mrs. Dorothy George has shown that the long-held belief that the Combination Laws were used in a grossly partial way against organizations of working-men is erroneous,[40] and it is the writer's impression that throughout the greater part of the nineteenth century the extent of combination of capitalists for the express purpose of settling wages was negligible. Adam Smith's contention was repeated by J. B. Say, but it did not pass without criticism. It was categorically denied in 1834, by E. C. Tufnell, a very able observer with an almost unrivalled knowledge of English industrial and labor conditions. "What may have been the case in the time of Adam Smith," he wrote, "we have no means of ascertaining, but certainly for a long period back there is no reason to suppose such a state of things to have existed."[41] Right through the century we find similar denials from trustworthy observers. The Committee on Artisans and Machinery of 1824 could find only one instance of a perfect combination of masters— twelve type-founders.[42] It is difficult at times to know what observers understood by "masters' combina-

40. *Econ. Jour. History Supp.*, 1927, p. 214.

41. *Character, Objects and Effects of Trade Unionism*, 1834, p. 99. Tufnell is criticizing the phrase about "tacit combination," but he undoubtedly had formal combinations in mind.

42. A great deal of further evidence could be brought forward to support this point, but an adequate analysis of it would necessitate lengthy treatment. (The Select Committee on Artisans and Machinery 1824; the Select Committee on the Combination Laws of 1825; and the Place Collection contain a large store of evidence on the point.)

tion."[43] Certainly, however, deliberately organized bodies on the lines of the unions were almost non-existent until late into the century. The early industrialists were imbued with a sturdy individualism that was repugnant to association. As Dr. Stirling pointed out: "The oft-quoted dictum of Adam Smith, that it is easy for a few capitalists to combine, is a grievous error . . . (they are) necessarily competitors, and therefore kept apart by natural rivalries."[44] "A combination of rival traders," said Buchanan, "is a phenomenon which, until human nature is changed, will never be exhibited."[45] "The same principle of selfishness which prompts them to form the league, prompts them also to break it. . . . Rival traders have no confidence in each other; no two of them will ever act in concert."[46] A similar attitude was taken by M'Culloch and others. Until the 'eighties this attitude was, to a superficial observer at any rate, correct. The aversion of employers to enter even into protective

---

43. There is no suggestion, of course, that the accounts of capitalist combination in the eighteenth and nineteenth centuries in Levy's *Monopolies, Trusts and Cartells* and other works are in any way misleading.

44. Stirling, *Trade Unionism*. Reprint from Second Edn. (1869), 1889, p. 40.

45. Buchanan's Editorial note to the *Wealth of Nations*, Vol. I, p. 210.

46. *Wealth of Nations*, Vol. I, pp. 206-7, note.

or defensive associations was brought out in evidence before the Trade Union Commission of 1867. That evidence suggested that the motive of employers' associations — reluctantly entered into — was self-defense. Very early in their history, combined workers had discovered the utility, as a coercive weapon, of the device so aptly named by the Webbs, "the strike in detail." Practically all the combinations among employers that were revealed by the inquiries in 1824 or 1825 were either retaliatory against unions exploiting "the strike in detail" or else the employers' side of "joint monopolies" operating with the encouragement and connivance of the workers. We shall discuss the latter later on. A good example of "the strike in detail" occurred immediately after the Repeal of the Combination Laws, when the Linen Weavers of Barnsley planned to compel workers, factory by factory, to strike, selecting the order by lot. The object was to coerce employers one by one, thus enabling the strikers to be supported out of contributions from those still working for other employers. The *Edinburgh Review*, commenting on this device in 1838, said that those who adopted it were generally victorious, and that this caused them to acquire the habit of considering themselves irresistible. "They produce," said the *Review*, "a universal conviction of the necessity of a combined resistance." Tufnell gave a description of the reluctant formation of a masters' association at Leeds following a strike in detail.[47] Many trustworthy observers gave this reason for such employers' combinations as then existed. In the middle of the century we find the same opinion held. W. L. Sargant, a student with an intimate knowledge of working-class movements, wrote in 1851: "I have shown that combinations among the men are inevitable, and where the workmen combine, masters will and must do the same."[48] In 1854 Morrison expressed a similar opinion and described the forms that employers' counter-combinations could take.[49] In the late 'sixties even trade-union advocates spoke of masters' associations as though they were *novelties*. "In the last dispute in the iron trade," said Longe, "employers taught an unruly and high-paid class of workmen the wholesome lesson that employers can combine as well as labourers."[50] Thornton, in a passage largely contradictory of other parts of his work, wrote: "Hitherto want of concert between individual masters has

---

47. Tufnell, *Character* . . . etc., pp. 101-2.
48. *Science of Social Opulence*, p. 404.
49. *On the Relations of Labour and Capital*, 1854, pp. 98-99.
50. *Refutation of the Wages Fund Theory*.

placed them at a great disadvantage as compared with the men," and "The lock-out is never initiative—it is always retaliatory."[51] Another friend of the unionists was sufficiently naïve to attribute inconsistency to employers *who during a strike* had entered into a combination "such as they did not hesitate to stigmatise in those who were not so well educated as themselves."[52] And the cry of an employer of about the same time has a sincere ring. "As yet war has only been declared on one side. . . . As yet capital has been passive, but it will not remain so long; it must soon, in self-defence, combine to defeat the tyranny of labour, and who then can doubt the result?"[53] The studies of Mr. W. Page for the period 1886 to 1890 seem to have suggested to him the same ephemeral and retaliatory character of employers' combinations. He states quite simply: "The combination for bargaining purposes of all classes of workers necessarily resulted in a like movement among the employers."[54] Contemporary observers of the rapidly developing trade-union movement in the British Dominions in the early 'nineties of last century

51. *On Labour*, Second Edn., 1870, p. 271.

52. Samuelson, *Friendly Hints to Trade Unionists*, 1867.

53. *Capital and Labour*, 1867. By a Member of the Manchester Chamber of Commerce.

54. *Commerce and Industry*, p. 333.

tell the same story. Referring to a great strike which had just failed owing to the employers getting together, a writer from Australia said that it proved that, "difficult as it was for employers to risk their rival interests against a common enemy, they will do so and receive public support in the most democratic countries, so long as labour makes a demand which the public holds to be arbitrary or unfair."[55] A New Zealand observer about the same time, writing on "Labour Troubles in New Zealand," declared that, apart from a shipowners' association "no other combination of employers was formed in this country until after the strike commenced. The natural conclusion is that the aggression of labour forced employers to combine in self-defence."[56]

THE QUESTION IS OF LESS SIGNIFICANCE IN MODERN TIMES

This rapid historical survey is based on a more or less arbitrary selection of opinions expressed by competent observers at different times during the last century. But again and again the writer has found evidence of the extreme reluctance with which competing interests have agreed to cooperate in their own defense and of the ephemeral nature of any

---

55. H. H. Champion, in *The Nineteenth Century*, Feb. 1891.
56. *Econ. Jour.*, 1891, p. 716.

associations which have thereby resulted. Since the late 'eighties other causes have led to the aggregation of capital on such a large scale that an inquiry as to whether employers' associations are primarily bodies which take initiative in labor questions or merely retaliatory, loses its significance.

JOINT SUPPORT BY OPPOSED COMBINATIONS

The motive for these combinations of masters was probably something more than mere direct defense, the opposing of the coercive device of "the strike" by that of the "lock-out." We have early evidence of workmen's societies being countenanced by the masters and used as instruments against factories which were "underselling." And we find unions claiming that their sole object was "to protect the upright manufacturer against the unfair competition of the avaricious one, and to secure a fair remuneration for labour."[57] But this very important phenomenon can be best discussed at a later stage.

"TACIT COMBINATION" BY MASTERS

Let us turn now to the rather vaguer but frequently quoted suggestion of Adam Smith's, that the employers were everywhere in a tacit but uni-

---

57. John Wade, *History of the Middle and Working Classes*, 1833, p. 284.

form combination to keep down wages. This has probably been more frequently quoted because, in its vagueness, it is more difficult to refute. It is quite understandable that in the time of Adam Smith masters had a kind of conception of the wages of a laborer as something definite, fixed and natural. Wages then varied slowly, and any master would naturally resent having to pay more than he had been accustomed to; but this would not prevent wages from rising. If there had been a tendency for wages to rise, it is quite certain that masters would have compared notes on meeting one another and complained of the iniquity of it. They would have done all in their power to avoid paying more; but the point is, could they have succeeded in keeping wages stationary? Pepys recorded how he paid his first maid three pounds a year and her clothes. A new cook who came later demanded four pounds, and he wrote: ". . . the first time I ever did give so much." Later still he wrote: "Wages are very considerable; a fat Welsh girl who has just come out of the country, scarce understood a word of English, capable of nothing but washing, scouring and sweeping the rooms . . . (received) six guineas a year, besides a guinea for her tea" (*Pepys' Diary*). And Defoe in 1725 deplored the fact that "women

servants are now so scarce that . . . their wages are
of late increased to six, seven, nay eight pounds per
annum and upwards. . . . But the greatest abuse of
all is that these creatures are become their own law-
givers; they hire themselves to you by their own
will. That is, a month's wages or a month's warning"
(*Everybody's Business, Nobody's Business*). However, the indignation and disgust of these gentlemen
did not enable them to escape paying the higher
wages caused by the scarcity; and we have no reason
to suppose that they acted any differently from other
masters of their day. It was the very futility of such
"tacit combinations" which led to the seventeenth-
century attempts to get the Justices to force maids
into service and to assess their wages.[58] And the
same thing applies to the alleged tacit combination
on the part of the farmers. The typical farmer is
still notoriously stupid over the matter of wages—
constantly complaining of the shortage of labor, and
when asked why he does not offer higher wages,
indignantly replying that laborers ought to be only
too grateful to get work at the wage he is offering.
But this spirit does not lower the price of labor: it
simply results in the farmer's demand being some-

---

58. E.g. See Brown, Bland & Tawney, *Select Documents* . . . ,
pp. 360, 361.

what less than it might otherwise be, for the shortage of which he complains remains. If he prefers that "shortage" to raising wages, presumably the existing rate is the economic one. Ultimately, all the dictum about a tacit combination comes to is that masters will not pay more than they believe to be necessary to get the labor they desire; and this does not operate solely on the employers' side. Laborers similarly will not offer to work for less than they believe they can get: the "Clay-Martin" Report of the South African Economic and Wage Commission 1925 alleges a tacit combination on the part of natives not to accept less than a certain rate of wages. This merely means that they know what they can get; the phrase simply sums up a typical attitude of mind, an attitude which may perhaps help to maintain stability or may act as an unavailing resistance to necessary change.[59]

THE MASTERS' NECESSITIES "NOT SO IMMEDIATE"

If the "tacit combination" theory exercised much influence because of its vagueness, still more does this seem to be the case with the third idea which

---

59. There is no suggestion, of course, that the psychological phenomenon of a group of competitors tacitly endeavoring "not to spoil" a buying or selling market (in a time of change) does not exist.

we have seen sprang from the *Wealth of Nations*.
To Adam Smith the masters had the advantage because their necessity for the men was "not so immediate" as that of the men for them, for while the
master could subsist for a long time upon stocks
acquired, many men "could not exist for a week, few
could subsist a month, and scarce any a year without employment." Although writing in the eighteenth
century he put it much more mildly than many modern writers, who talk as though any unemployed
worker is faced with immediate starvation. We must
remember, however, that this idea was held by Smith
as a sort of appurtenance to and amplification of his
subsistence theory which, as has already been shown,
was quite erroneous and, moreover, apparently given
up by himself. The theory was kept alive in a general way by the Socialists, whose "exploitation theory"
may have been the source from which the idea was
so strongly reinforced in the late 'sixties. "Who so
blind," said Louis Blanc, "as not to see that, under
its domination (competition), the continuous fall of
wages, far from being exceptional, is necessarily universal." Many of the economists who condemned the
exploitation theory put forward, nevertheless, the
rather milder theory of "the employers' advantage";
and it appears as if they were not uninfluenced by

it. The theory of the employers' advantage causes the worker, as one writer put it, to visualize the capitalist as a "Gulliver of labour, only to be mastered by the united efforts of Lilliputian numbers."[60] It is surprising that the idea obtained such a wide acceptance. Appeal to facts could have given little support to it. "Nine-tenths of the cotton-workers," said Tufnell, criticizing the theory, "never think of forming Unions, and the alleged advantage has never been taken of them."[61] Said another writer: To tell a "baffled contractor" wanting to get labor that "nothing but a close combination" can give workers "even a chance of successfully contending with employers must sound in his ears like dismal mockery."[62] And in the words of yet another critic: "The labourer . . . is at no disadvantage in bargaining with the employer, who is tied to his machines, which he must keep fully employed, or perish financially."[63] In the writings of Thornton and the other authors of the late 'sixties mentioned above, attempts to justify or rationalize the theory took various forms, only some of which is it worth while examining. As

---

60. Stirling, "Mr. Mill on Trades Unions," in *Recess Studies,* 1870, p. 317.

61. *Character* . . . etc., *op. cit.,* p. 96.

62. Stirling, *op. cit.,* p. 319.

63. Cree, *op. cit.,* p. 20.

has been suggested, these attempts appear to be little
more than inventions of vague phrases, which, if
conveying a clear meaning to some economists, have
served as mere catchwords and substitutes for thinking by others.

"ON TERMS OF EQUALITY"

One of the most common is that combination puts
the worker "on terms of equality" or "on an equal
footing" with the employer; it gives him "equality
of bargaining strength."[64] Can we give any definite
meaning to this term "equality"? Thornton tried to.
He took an example of a product created by the
joint contributions of one worker and one employer
and assumed that if they were on "an equal footing"
the product would be divided equally between them.
This is so absurd that one wonders that he ever
allowed it to get into print, but it gave him an oppor-
tunity of himself criticizing the vague phrases used
by others. He thought that he had dealt with it satis-
factorily merely by contradicting it. "Nothing is
easier than to show," he added, "that if labourers
were really on the same footing as their employers,

---

64. The use of the terms "strong" and "weak" in economic literature was criticized by Pantaleoni in the *Economic Journal*,
1898, p. 193.

the equality between them would after all be but a sham and a cloak for the extremest inequality."[65]

THE WORKER "HAS NO RESERVE"

The idea is made a little more explicit when it is developed into the theory that the worker is at a disadvantage because he has no reserve. The derivation from Adam Smith is obvious. The capitalist "has the advantage of past accumulations in striking his bargain" runs the formula; he can "discharge a single workman with comparatively slight inconvenience, while the workman loses the whole means of subsistence."[66] The employer, it is held, "can generally wait longer for labour than labourers can wait for wages. . . . This is why the price of labour is generally so much depressed."[67]

EXAGGERATIONS AND CONFUSIONS INTRODUCED BY THESE IDEAS

Without the subsistence theory to rest upon such conceptions appear to be the emptiest of sophisms. Sometimes Smith's moderate dictum about the relative urgencies of the master's and workman's neces-

---

65. Thornton, *op. cit.*, p. 192.
66. "Committee on Trade Societies of the Nat. Assn. for the Prom. of Soc. Sci." in *Transactions*, 1860.
67. Thornton, *op. cit.*, p. 175.

sities is exaggerated into the statement that the latter must take whatever the employer offers or starve. Thornton, trying to justify this view, was led into the wildest exaggerations. He contended first that the individual laborer could not "carry his labour to a better market or spare the time to go elsewhere," a contention that the slightest examination of the labor mobility of his day would have upset; and to this argument he added, that savings would avail him little.[68] Possibly, he had noticed that workers with savings were getting no more wages for the same work than those without, but with this admission what becomes of the "labourer has no reserve" theory? We are forced to the conclusion that there is some distinction between collective saving by the union and individual saving, or that individual reserve funds are no reserves at all. If this is the case, Thornton's attempted expansion and generalization of the particular theory also falls to the ground. "Price," he said, "in any particular instance will be greater or less according as it is the buyer or seller who is best in a position to take advantage of the other's necessities."[69] But the only explicit meaning given for

68. *Ibid.*, p. 102.
69. *Ibid.*, p. 143.

"necessities" is lack of a reserve, so that if savings "avail little" the whole idea is meaningless. If the argument had been that poverty acted as a restriction on the mobility of the laborer, and so prevented him from selling his services in the most profitable market, it would have appeared more plausible. There is a suspicion of this idea in the passage just quoted, but it is confused with the "reserve fund" idea, and suggests that the disadvantage arising from lack of mobility can be overcome without restoring mobility. Surely the plain truth is that we can make no useful generalizations on this matter at all. It might be argued with equal justification that the worker without savings has an advantage over the worker with savings because he has nothing to lose.

THE "DEPENDENCE" AND "INSECURITY" OF THE WORKER

Most writers who use these ideas are less explicit than Thornton, and so less easy to criticize. With some, the worker's disadvantage seems to be implicit in the relationship of "employer and employed" (as it is called), and the alleged "dependence" of the worker resulting therefrom. The phrase "employer and employed" is in itself greatly misleading, for the ultimate employers of labor are the consumers, and it is on their demand that the workers are dependent.[70] The development of this relationship did not bring, however, any obvious new disadvantages. On the contrary, the *security* of the working class was greatly increased. The *Edinburgh Review* in 1837 could speak about "the comparatively perfect security of the working classes in later times"; and Nicholson could point out, towards the end of the century, that "the wage-earners of this country as a whole . . . have a much more stable income than the mass of peasant proprietors in other countries; the yield to labour on the large system of industry is much more *certain* than the yield to land of the *petite culture*."[71] There is no reason for supposing that the relationship of the wage-earner to society is less stable than that of the poor proprietor.

CONTRADICTION OF THESE IDEAS BY "THE PIN MONEY" ARGUMENT

It is enlightening to oppose to these arguments another one, curiously enough often naïvely used by the same writers, which completely contradicts them. It argues that the possession of a reserve, or the relative *absence* of necessities (i.e., a lower con-

---

70. See Cannan, *Review of Economic Theory*, pp. 433-443.
71. *Econ. Jour.*, 1892, p. 482.

ventional standard of life), far from causing higher wages to come to the possessor, leads to lower wages. In one of its forms it is sometimes called "the pin money" argument. The contention is that those who have some other source of income or some alternative income can, on this account, have their wages forced down. In another of its forms it might be called "the standard of living theory of wages." The suggestion is that a certain body of workers (usually alien immigrants or non-white residents among European peoples), on account of their being accustomed to a lower standard of living, find themselves earning lower wages. They get less, it is said, because they have fewer requirements. According to the particular sentiment attaching to the people concerned, we are either told that they are "exploited" or that they are themselves the evil party in persisting in undercutting. But the economics of the phenomenon are wholly explicable in terms of the effect of the characteristics of the workers upon their supply.

LABOR SOLD "WITHOUT RESERVE"

Thornton put forward also a rather different form of the conception of the laborer's lack of a reserve. He declared that the price of labor was determined on different principles from that of other commodities because it was "sold without reserve." "Isolated labour," he said, "is almost always sold without reserve, whereas tangible commodities are scarcely ever so sold." How is it that high prices are secured? "Plainly, by not selling unreservedly." That is true enough if it merely means that some part of the supply is held back; but as will be seen when we come to the form of the theory which says that "labor is perishable," the phrase is probably based on fallacious reasoning. Even Mill, who showered extravagant praise on Thornton's book, pointed out that "reserving a price is, to all intents and purposes, withdrawing supply."[72] The most careful analysis does not reveal ~~that it means anything more than~~ that it means anything more than that uncombined labor cannot exploit monopoly power. Quite often this is clearly all that is meant when it is said that the workers are "at the employers' mercy." For example, the executive of an American trade union declares that if skilled work could be obtained without the necessity of years of experience, "any craft would be thrown open to the competition of an almost unlimited labour supply; and the craftsmen in it would be practically at the mercy of the employer."[73]

---

72. *Fortnightly Review,* 1869.
73. Quoted in L. C. Marshall, *Industrial Society,* p. 562.

LABOR IS "A PERISHABLE COMMODITY"

Another form taken by the idea that labor is exploited because it cannot wait is that which says that labor is a perishable commodity. We have to thank or blame Thornton for this form of the idea. "Labour," he said, ". . . will not *keep*." Criticism soon came.[74] Even General Walker, who believed that in his final overthrow of the wage-fund theory he had provided a justification of trade unionism, attacked the idea. His criticism was not altogether satisfactory. It was based partly upon a hair-splitting point about time spent in rest not resulting in waste, but in labor being "stored up,"[75] and partly upon a contention that the buyer of labor was in precisely the same position.[76] "If he does not buy today's labour today," wrote Walker, "he surely can not buy it tomorrow"; and he went on to say that with a cessation of industry the employer would become "industrially defunct" when he had eaten up his capital, whereas the laborer in "preserving his thews and sinews preserved also his stock in trade and his industrial ability." A criticism by Nicholson in 1892 went nearer to the point. ". . . A man who cannot

---

74. Cairnes criticized the theory privately to Thornton.
75. *The Wages Question*, 1876, p. 292.
76. *Ibid.*, p. 294.

employ his capital," he wrote, "loses his income as surely as a labourer out of work loses his wages. . . . If the one is perishable, so is the other. We are constantly reminded that a labourer is liable to dismissal, and thus indirectly to starvation and death. But though this may be true of a labourer it is not true of labour. To say that all the labour of a country, or even a considerable part, could be dismissed by capital, is palpably absurd."[77] By all odds the best criticism came from Pierson. "Thornton's argument," he pointed out, "is defective. The 'keeping' of labour—supposing it could be kept—would not diminish the supply of labour; it would simply delay it. At a given moment there would be fewer people offering to sell their labour; but their number would be all the greater later on. Organisation in a particular trade is capable of achieving its purposes, because, in a particular trade, it is capable of permanently limiting the supply of labour. But this limitation leads to an increase in the supply of labour in other trades; and if all work-people were organised, the conditions under which alone a Trade Union can exercise a permanent influence upon the rate of wages would nowhere be fulfilled."[78] One would

---

77. *Econ. Jour.*, 1892, p. 480.
78. Pierson, *Principles*, Vol. I, p. 270.

have thought, after such criticism as Pierson's, that the phrase "labor will not keep" would have disappeared for ever from the economic text-books; but it cheerfully persists. Marshall continued to explain that labor was at a disadvantage in bargaining because it was "perishable."[79] Probably through his influence the idea has become sanctified in current economic jargon;[80] thousands of students have repeated it parrot-wise in examinations; and when Mr. R. G. Hawtrey in 1926 ornaments the idea with flowers and epigram we do not feel shocked. "What he withholds today," says Mr. Hawtrey, "cannot be sold tomorrow, for labour is more perishable than cut flowers. Tomorrow, today's labour will no longer exist."[81] He does not merely mean that if the laborer (from his own fault or owing to the defects of eco-

---

79. Marshall, *Principles*, Third Edn., p. 647.

80. The extent of the hold which this idea possesses is seen in the erroneous attributing of the phrase: that "a strike fund would make labour less perishable, and therefore, as far as bargaining strength was concerned, more on a par with capital," to a workman in 1831. See the Economic History Supplement of the *Economic Journal*, No. 3, p. 388. The passage in the *Cambrian* (1st October, 1831) on which the above words are based reads as follows: ". . . that if they had been associated with the clubs in time past, they might have opposed a reduction in wages and obtained relief if the attempts to reduce (wages) had been persisted in."

81. Hawtrey, *The Economic Problem*, p. 29.

nomic organization) does not work, the time he has wasted cannot be regained. He holds that because the worker cannot acquire an accumulated stock of his labor and defer selling when the market seems to require it "he is only too likely to sell his services at a price below that which the market, properly approached, might yield him."[82]

THE SURVIVAL OF THE "SUBSISTENCE THEORY"

The persistence of all these theories seems to be in part due to the survival of the subsistence theory superstition, the idea that wages tend "naturally" or through competition to fall to "the lowest point" or "a minimum," although as we have seen, Adam Smith gave no logical explanation for the belief, but merely assumed that because wages could not be below that level they could not be above. Thornton and Mill, we have seen, were influenced by it. Even Walker was led by a similar kind of belief to justify unionism. He argued first that *imperfect competition*, which operated against the worker, might lead to a disadvantageous bargain in the first place and that the low wage resulting would become perpetuated through

---

82. Mr. Hawtrey's discussion involves a point about the worker's disadvantage in not being "a specialist in the art of selling," and the phrase "properly approached" may have had the whole of this idea in mind. In essence, however, the argument appears to be the same as that which Pierson criticized.

consequent inefficiency. In such circumstances, he said, there was no "tendency in any economical forces to repair the mischief." After an illustration of how this worked he brought in a theory of a different kind. Not only was there no tendency in purely economic forces to right the evil, but they themselves tended to perpetuate it. "Such disasters aside," he said (referring to his illustration), "the tendency of purely economical forces is continually to aggravate the disadvantages from which any person or class may suffer. . . . Every gain which one party makes at the expense of another, provides the thews and sinews of war for further aggressions."[83] Yet, like other economists, Walker probably had misgivings on this subject, as evidenced by his reversing the *apparent* original meaning of the passage last quoted in the otherwise identical passage in his *Political Economy*, published later. He inserted the words: "under impaired competition," which considerably weakened the suggestion that purely economic forces tend to perpetuate rather than to counteract the results of originally disadvantageous bargains.[84] Out-

---

83. *The Wages Question*, pp. 165-166.
84. The revised passage reads: "Irrespective of anything catastrophic, the tendency of purely economic forces, under impaired competition, is continually to aggravate the disadvantages, etc." (*Political Economy*, Third Edition, p. 265.)

side the ranks of the more orthodox economists we find a host of prolific writers who have blamed competition itself rather than its impairment, for "the tendency of wages to a minimum." The idea probably found its crudest expression in the writings of Charles Kingsley and the Christian Socialists, and undoubtedly exercised a great deal of influence through the anti-sweating movements. It has received lengthy and deliberate treatment in the Webbs' *Industrial Democracy*, and is one of the main bases of their advocacy of unionism. Marshall's treatment of the idea certainly did not give authority to the view that "economic forces" or competition tended to depress the worker, but it was similar to Walker's in holding that the disadvantageous position of the worker was cumulative. "It lowers his wages," he wrote, "and as we have seen, this lowers his efficiency as a worker, and thereby lowers the normal value of his labour."[85] This amounts to saying that there is a dynamic force tending to cause wages to fall through the decreased efficiency of labor. Views of this sort are popular, but are usually accepted very uncritically. Economists have always noticed that where the standard of living is low there is low efficiency; and there is no doubt that a low stand-

---

85. Marshall, *Principles*, Third Edn., p. 649.

ard of living is often an important factor causing that low efficiency; but this does not in itself allow that there is a dynamic tendency downwards. Surely this generalization puts the cart before the horse. In so far as low wages are due to inefficiency, from whatever cause, the right thing to do is to tackle that inefficiency directly. Interference with the price mechanism seems to be the very worst way of trying to deal with it. There is, however, no theoretical solution to this particular question—it must be answered by appeal to experience; and yet, if there were anything in the idea, would not employers have discovered it? Few of them are unaware of the effect on efficiency of the stimulus of piece work, of making increased income the certain reward of improved efficiency. May not their general doubt that increased reward will automatically bring greater efficiency be due to the simple fact that in general it does not?

PART TWO

Indeterminateness

IN THE LATE 'SIXTIES what appears to have been an entirely new idea was brought into the discussion of collective bargaining. It seems to consist in the rationalization of an idea which had for long vaguely existed in "the untutored mind of the workman," but which previous economists, according to Edgeworth, had wrongly condemned as fallacious. The workman knew that if he argued and haggled with a shopkeeper about the price of an article he might obtain it for less than its marked price; and on this analogy, he did not see why, by threatening to strike, he should not obtain more wages for his labor. This theme was borrowed by the economists and developed by them into a theory that the price of labor was indeterminate, and that within the range of its indeterminateness trade unionism had a legitimate field of action, in the same way that there was a valid field for haggling in the indeterminateness of barter. It was towards this notion that Thornton, Jenkin, Longe and Leslie were in fact confusedly groping—towards a conception of the indeterminateness that exists under conditions that we now call "bi-lateral monopoly." Their groping was very blind, for competition on both sides (not monopoly) was generally blamed for labor's disadvantageous bargain.

FORMERLY, THE INDEFINITENESS OF ISOLATED BARGAINS SEEMS TO HAVE BEEN THOUGHT UNIMPORTANT

The earlier economists appeared to assume, either tacitly or expressly, that the indefiniteness of any particular bargain was of no importance. They were merely concerned with market-price, which they regarded as both the resultant of the innumerable individual bargains and the index of the level to which all prices would tend, and from which, in the presence of competition, they could not greatly diverge. Longfield, for instance, started with the case of barter, but did not think it worth while analyzing, as "In all civilised societies goods are exchanged for money or sold." Moreover, while he recognized quite clearly the opposition of interest which led every individual "to buy as cheap and to sell as dear" as he could, he did not go to the trouble of pointing out the possible ratios of exchange which could arise in any individual case, because in fact, we have "the law of mutual competition."[86] Some degree of freedom of competition he seemed to take as axiomatic. "As this state of freedom nearly exists in all civilised countries," he wrote (after a reference to the forces in the labor market), "the principle just mentioned is not to be considered as a hypothetical axiom, but both it and the consequences drawn from it are truths of considerable importance."[87] In a hypothetical isolated case, he knew that the result of a bargain between two people would be *indeterminate*, although he did not use this word; but the ratio resulting from that theoretical example had no relation to any rate that would be established in practice. "A labourer working for himself," he wrote, "would find it to his interest to give 19/20ths of the produce of his labour to the person who would lend him (a spade), if the alternative was that he should turn up the earth with his naked hands." But this rate is not paid because of the competition of capital for employment and because the profits of the least-paid capital "regulate the profits of the rest."[88] A writer in a later age might have expressed the same thought

86. *Lectures on Politicial Economy*, 1834, p. 46.
87. *Ibid.*, p. 67.
88. *Ibid.*, p. 195.

more clearly, perhaps, by saying that, whatever the "curve of indifference" of the laborer might be, he would not have to pay more than the market price for the use of capital. Neither profits nor wages, he thought, were determined by the "intensity of demand," which is "the sacrifice we would make to obtain any commodity, if the alternative were to be compelled to remain without it."[89] Longfield has been quoted at length because he was here deliberately setting on one side as unimportant, ideas which were later thought to be novel, revolutionary and fundamental. And his judgment seems to have been right.

THE EVOLUTION OF THE IDEA

The first clear statement of the "indeterminateness" idea the writer has found in English economic literature is in a paper read to the Royal Statistical Society in 1867 by one Jacob Waley. He argued that the sharing of the gross returns of industry between capital and labor would be "in a perpetual flux and never have time to settle into a state of stable equilibrium. . . ." He continued: "I conceive that there will in general be a large margin of uncertainty as to the division of the returns, and that the precise place at which the line is drawn will to a very con-

89. *Ibid.,* p. 194.

siderable extent be determined by circumstances which may fairly be called fortuitous, and may be greatly influenced by a bargain between the employer and the employed." In such a case it was quite possible that a strike would be successful. This is as clear and as moderate a statement of the theory as is to be found anywhere. There are passages in F. D. Longe's essay which suggest that he had the idea in mind, and Fleeming Jenkin in 1868 had some conception of it. (We cannot here discuss the several interesting fallacies in Jenkin's able work.) He said that the division of the produce between capital and labor was "purely a question of bargain"; and it could legitimately vary "within very wide limits."[90] In 1869 Thornton helped to spread the idea by a violent yet vague attack on supply and demand generally (*On Labour . . .* , 1869).[91] At times, when reading his book, one imagines that he must have regarded the price mechanism as a completely arbitrary affair; but the work is so full of apparent contradictions that one can never be sure of his real meaning. (We are giving so much attention to Thornton because of the extent of his influ-

90. Fleeming Jenkin, *Collected Papers*, p. 22.
91. At first published as articles, then incorporated in *On Labour . . .* , 1869. Two Editions.

ence on this topic and because his contribution received extravagant praise from Mill.) "The price,
whether of labour or anything else, in no case what-
soever depends upon the proportion between supply and demand,"[92] was his contention. "The propo-
sitions of supply and demand do not hold good under
ordinary circumstances."[93] For supply and demand
he substituted "competition," which would suggest
a mere verbal quibble; but he asked: "What regu-
lates competition?" (p. 79) and replied: "Nothing.
There is no regularity about competition—competition is not regulated at all . . . there is no law of
competition," (p. 80). We cannot follow him into
the arguments which led him to this strange conclusion, but the notion seems to have arisen out of
his expansion of a few special and for the most part
quite unlikely cases into generalizations. This is so
in spite of the fact that he claimed to have covered
nearly the whole field of possible cases with his
examples. Mill did not fail to see this point; he admitted that most of the examples were, "on the face
of them, altogether exceptional,"[94] but it was out of

92. *Ibid.*, Second Edn., p. 44.
93. *Ibid.*, p. 49.
94. *Fortnightly Review*, 1869—reprinted in *Essays and Disserta-
tions*, Vol. IV.

a criticism of some of Thornton's illustrations that he developed his theory of indeterminateness.

THE PROBABLE FIRST USE OF THE WORD "INDETERMINATENESS" IN THIS CONNECTION

One of Thornton's arguments was illustrated by an auction; and he showed how the price at which a particular article would actually exchange hands might be different according to whether bidding was up or down. Mill pointed out that to establish the point of this example he had to suppose "the case to be an exception to the rule that demand increases with cheapness: and since this rule, though general, is not absolutely universal he is scientifically right . . . but . . . in the general market of the world—it is the next thing to impossible that more of the commodity should not be asked for at every reduction of the price." In spite of this severe criticism he admitted that Thornton had "proved that the law of supply and demand is not the whole theory of the particular case . . . what he has shown is that the law is, in this particular case, consistent with two different prices, and is equally and completely filled by either of them. The demand and supply are equal at 20s. and equal also at 18s. The conclusion is not that the law is false . . . the phenomenon cannot help obeying it, but there is some amount of indeterminateness in its operation, a certain limited extent of variation is possible within the bounds of the law. . . ." This is probably the first use of the word "indeterminateness" in this sense.[95]

CASES WHICH THE SUPPLY AND DEMAND DOCTRINE OF PRICE "DOES NOT REACH"

Mill then went on seriously to discuss some of Thornton's other examples, to show that the laws of supply and demand still stood. He gravely pointed out, for instance, that in one case "at £50 there is a demand for twice or three times the supply; at £50 0s. 0¼d. there is no demand at all. When the scale of demand is broken by so extraordinary a jump the law fails of its application. . . ." And in another case he remarked: "Here, again, the author is obliged to suppose that the whole body of customers (24 in number) place the extreme limit of what they are prepared to pay rather than go without the article exactly at the same point . . . the case is just possible in a very small market—practically impossible in the great market of the community." Nevertheless, from these examples Mill reached the conclusion: "when the equation of demand and supply leaves

_____
95. Thornton had used the word "indeterminateness" in regard to the size of the wage-fund.

the price in part indeterminate, because there is more than one price which would fulfil the law, neither buyers nor sellers are under the action of any motives derived from supply and demand to give way to one another." The doctrine Thornton had tried to controvert, though true, was not the whole truth. "He has shown," said Mill, "and has been the first to show, that there are cases which it does not reach."

THE CRUCIAL POINT

This brings us to the crucial point in the whole of Mill's argument. "If it should turn out," he wrote, "that the price of labour falls within one of the excepted cases—the case which the law of equality between demand and supply does not provide for, because several prices all agree in satisfying that law —we are able to see that the question between one of these prices and another will be determined by causes which operate strongly against the labourer, and in favour of the employer." After discussing this possibility he remembered the "If" and wrote: "It will of course be said that these speculations are idle, for labour is not in that barely possible excepted case." That is just what would occur to one and what one would expect him to prove. But he made no attempt at a proof. Instead, he went off into a criticism of the wage-fund doctrine and, leaping over an immense logical gap, wrote: "There is no law of nature making it inherently impossible for wages to rise to the point of absorbing not only the funds which he had intended to devote to carrying on his business, but the whole of what he allows for his private expenses, beyond the necessaries of life." He obviously believed that in having shown that the conception of fixed limits to the wage-fund was erroneous he had shown that a huge range of indeterminateness existed, the exact limits of which he defined more carefully later as "the highest wages consistent with keeping up the capital of the country and increasing it *pari passu* with the increase of the people, and the lowest that will enable the labourers to keep up their numbers with an increase sufficient to provide labourers for the increase of employment." This compares strangely with the moderation of his earlier generalization: "There is some amount of indeterminateness in its action, a certain limited amount of variation is possible within the bounds of the law." Thus, with no possible justification of any kind, with absolutely no logical foundation whatever, he declared that Thornton had shown that "the doctrine hitherto taught by all or most economists (including himself) which denied it to be possible that trade unions can raise wages . . . is deprived of its scientific foundation and must be thrown aside."

DIAGRAMMATIC TREATMENT

There were similar ideas, as has been mentioned, in an essay by Fleeming Jenkin published before Thornton's book. After Mill's article had appeared and after a correspondence with Jevons, Jenkin developed his ideas in a further essay, and it is probable that, through its influence on Edgeworth (and Jevons), his work had more to do with the perpetuation of the idea of indeterminateness than Mill's. Already, in 1868, Jenkin had expressed the equation of supply and demand algebraically, and in 1870 he introduced, independently of the then forgotten Cournot, and Dupuit, the device of supply and demand curves. It is not hard to imagine that such a writer should have profoundly interested the leading mathematical economist of the past generation. Edgeworth gave the two essays most enthusiastic praise, and as it was he who, more than any other thinker, elaborated the theory of indeterminateness, we can probably trace the cause to Jenkin. He (Jenkin) illustrated by supply and demand curves Thornton's example of price in an auction, to which we have

already referred, and showed that it really made the
simple assumption that demand in the neighborhood
of the market price was constant at all prices; that
is, the demand curve became horizontal[96] near the
market price and, owing to the supply curve also
being level (one quantity offered singly and without
reserve), the actual market price would be indeterminate. He described the diagram as representing "an
unusual state of mind." This is putting it mildly indeed. It depends entirely upon the fortuitous coincidence of the horizontal section of an unusual and
highly improbable demand curve with an absolutely
rigid supply curve. Had the supply been larger or
smaller to any noticeable extent, even in this example,
the price would have been theoretically determinate.
Developing this idea and, it seems, getting further
away from economic realities, he said: "Where only
a small number of transactions take place there can
. . . be no theoretical market price; thus, with one
buyer and seller of one thing, the demand and supply curve become two straight lines. . . . If the supply
line overlaps the demand line, the sale will take place,
and not otherwise; but the price is indeterminate."[97]

---

96. He represented prices on the horizontal axis.
97. Fleeming Jenkin, *Collected Papers,* p. 85.

EDGEWORTH DEVELOPED THE IDEA, BUT LATER ON SEEMS TO HAVE DOUBTED ITS IMPORTANCE

This was the idea that Edgeworth developed and the one that led him to make the remark already quoted, possibly inspired by the similar remark by Mill to the effect that the old belief that trade unions could not raise wages had to be given up. We cannot here discuss the detailed development of the idea in his hands. His chief contribution to the theory was to draw curves of indifference for two bargainers, thus representing graphically the area of indeterminateness. But he did not, any more than did Mill, show that there was any justification for considering the value of labor as specially influenced by this principle, or that it disclosed any increment of the total product of industry which could be diverted to those who provided labor. We cannot be certain as to how far the Edgeworth of 1891 would have upheld the point of view expressed in 1881, for in a criticism of Marshall's "Note on Barter" (The "Note on Barter" appeared in the Second Edition of Marshall's *Principles*), he said, after an analysis of ideas of which he was the chief original propagator, that in comparison with other conditions of the labor market, they were "of little practical importance."

In his own words: "I do not, however, regard these nice points as more than *curiosa*, of little practical importance in comparison with the conditions of the labour market on which Marshall has dwelt." He referred here to "the tendency of any accidental disadvantage under which the work-people may be suffering to become perpetuated through the lowering of their vitality and efficiency."[98] This, however, is an entirely different point. Edgeworth had completely changed the basis of his defense of unionism. That same year, in his Introductory Lecture on Political Economy at Oxford, he said: "As an instance in which eminent theorists may have omitted a relevant circumstance, may be taken the question whether it is possible for trade unionists, by standing out for a higher than the market rate of wages, to benefit themselves permanently without injuring other workmen. The negative answer which has sometimes been given omits the consideration that an increase of wages tends to increase efficiency . . . etc." This deliberately avoids a reference to the affirmative answer which he had given ten years previously. In Sidgwick's *Principles*, Mr. L. L. Price's *Industrial Peace,* and Prof. Pigou's *Principles and Methods of*

---

98. Edgeworth, *Papers Relating to Political Economy*, Vol. II, p. 319.

Industrial Peace, the idea *seems* to have survived with more importance than Edgeworth would himself have attached to it.

MR. FLUX HAS DOUBTED ITS IMPORTANCE

We can detect in other economists who have dealt with the question the same doubt as to the importance of the idea. Mr. Flux, for example, discussing the alleged indeterminate increment, in 1900[99] wrote: "Now, it can not be denied that this element is in existence in fact. The question rather is, whether it has sufficient generality, and whether the relative importance of the amounts involved in such as may entitle it to figure prominently in a discussion of the general problem of distribution."[100]

MARSHALL'S TREATMENT

The later treatment of the idea by Marshall is very uncertain compared to his earlier treatment of it. He was possibly the first to give an even superficially satisfactory explanation of why the value of labor should be considered as specially influenced by this principle. Basing his treatment on Edgeworth's conception, he illustrated it by considering the extremely

99. *Econ. Jour.*, 1900, p. 381.
100. Compare Edgeworth's review of Davidson's "Bargain Theory of Wages" in the *Economic Journal*, 1899.

artificial cases of the barter, in isolation, of nuts and apples. In such an example he had no difficulty in showing "the uncertainty of the rate at which equilibrium is reached." It is what we should expect in a case of simple barter. But in the earlier editions of his *Principles* he said that this uncertainty "Does not depend on the fact that one commodity is being bartered for another instead of being sold for money. It results from our being obliged to regard the marginal utilities of both commodities as varying" (Third Edn., p. 415). It was *this* consideration that caused him to regard the price as likely to be indeterminate and arrived at *as* under barter, although, in fact, not a subject of barter. After his general treatment of the temporary equilibrium of demand and supply he remarked: "We did not allow for any appreciable change in the marginal utility of money . . . (which is) justifiable with regard to most of the markets with which we are practically concerned. . . . The exceptions are rare and unimportant in markets for commodities; but in markets for labour they are frequent and important. When a workman is in fear of hunger, the marginal utility of money to him is very high; and if at starting he gets the worst of the bargaining and is employed at low wages, it remains low, and he may go on selling his labour at a low rate" (pp. 411, 412, Third Edn.). This led him to his discussion of the barter of nuts and apples with a view of "throwing additional light" on the problem. In spite of the contention by Edgeworth that this treatment of "the specific peculiarities of the labour market . . . left little to be said freshly"[101] we find Marshall's doubts expressed in subsequent changes of text. In a later edition he had substituted throughout for the workman's "marginal utility of money," "his need of money (its marginal utility to him)" (Seventh Edn.). This is a strange amendment, for while the word "need" is vague, "marginal utility" is definite. He probably felt that the phrase "*his* marginal utility" did not quite fit the case. However, in a later edition he had relegated his "Note on Barter" to the Appendix and omitted the phrase which claimed that it threw "additional light" on the labor market. (Compare p. 412, Third Edn. and p. 336, Seventh Edn.) This also suggests a change of attitude. But his amendment to the "Note on Barter" was such as amounted to a tacit renunciation of the whole previous argument. Instead of contending that indeterminateness "does not depend on the fact that one commodity is being bartered for another instead of being sold for money," he seemed completely to

---

101. *Econ. Jour.*, 1899, p. 231.

reverse his previous content, and said that it "depends indirectly on the fact that one commodity is being bartered for another instead of being sold for money . . . the steadying influences which hold together a market in which values are set in money are absent" (Seventh Edn., p. 793).[102] All the amended argument of the later editions comes to is this; that where there is buying and selling through the agency of money there is more likely to be an effective market. Absence of money economy is one factor which may cause market forces to be ineffective.

UNDER COMPETITION, THE MARGINAL UTILITIES OF "INCOME" OR "MONEY" ARE IRRELEVANT TO THIS PROBLEM

Having made the uncertainty of the equilibrium rates depend upon barter (and ultimately, though not *expressly* stated, upon the absence of an effective market), any peculiarities of labor in respect of the marginal utility of money become irrelevant. We get back to the position that Longfield discussed a century ago. An individual worker's need for income might be so great that he would be prepared to give 19/20ths of the results of his labor to the

---

102. The word "indirectly" seems the wrong one. If he had said "generally" it would have been more true; for indeterminateness can exist where all transactions take place through the monetary mechanism.

person who would lend him a spade rather than till
the soil with his hands. But the market rate might be
such that he might have to give only 1/5th. It is
quite true that the poorer a workman is, the higher
will be the marginal utility to him of further increments of income—that is, of those commodities in
general which satisfy his needs; but while it is clear
that that will affect the intensity or amount of his
efforts to get further income we have no reason at
all to suppose that it will (*a*) prevent in any way the
formation of an effective market for his labor, (*b*)
cause an equilibrium in the market at a lower rate
than would result from the same quantity of labor
being offered by workers to whom the marginal
utilities of income were lower.

JEVONS' TREATMENT IN "THE THEORY OF POLITICAL ECONOMY"

With Jevons the theory developed in a rather different way. Like Edgeworth he seems to have been
influenced by Thornton and Jenkin. The latter had
corresponded with him on the subject of the mathematical treatment of economics before publishing his
second article, and it was partly in consequence of
Jenkin's essays that Jevons decided to put his own
Theory of Political Economy into print as early as
1871. The idea emerged in his treatment of the theory

of exchange. He put forward the proposition that "the equation of exchange will fail to be possible when the commodity or useful article possessed on one or both sides is indivisible . . ." as, for instance, in the case of a house,[103] "because we cannot contemplate the existence of an increment or decrement to an indivisible article.[104] . . . The theory seems to give a very unsatisfactory answer, for the problem proves to be, within certain limits, indeterminate." Such a bargain, he said, "must be settled upon other than strictly economic grounds." What *would* determine the result was "the comparative amount of knowledge of each other's *position* and *needs* (our italics) which each bargainer may possess." The only meaning we can suggest for this phrase is that the seller will endeavor to find out how the utility to be derived by the prospective buyer from the house compares with the utility he can derive by spending an equal amount in available alternative ways. What one is prepared to give for any commodity (or increment of a commodity) is a function of alternatives or alternative sources of supply. But Jevons was tacitly

---

103. The example of the sale of an estate was discussed in a not dissimilar manner in T. J. Dunning's *Trade Unions and Strikes* . . . , 1859, p. 6.

104. As a matter of fact, it is very easy to conceive of an increment to a house, as, indeed, of most other large properties.

assuming that there *were* no alternative sources of supply of houses. The case is similar to the theoretically isolated transaction which we saw Longfield had dismissed as of no practical importance. It rests on three assumptions—largeness of unit, uniqueness and monopoly. The general unimportance of the idea is further brought out in his elaboration of it. He held that indeterminateness existed even when commodities were divisible, if their divisibility was not into infinitely small quantities. As an illustration, he took bottles of ink. A fixed price (presumably competitive) of one shilling each was given, and the indeterminateness thrown on to quantity—that is, the number of bottles purchased at that price. Would the last and doubtful one be purchased? Here, again, these hypothetical transactions are isolated both in space and time. Putting aside the absence of competing ink supplies, or supplies available in different-sized units, when we take the factor of *time* into account, we see that the size of the unit purchased at a particular transaction loses all its relevance and importance. We can only imagine the size of the bottles affecting the interval between purchases—not the amount of ink consumed. This has an obvious parallel, as we shall see, in the case of the supply of some kinds of capital equipment.

THE DANGER OF GENERALIZING FROM ISOLATED CASES, AND IGNORING THE TIME FACTOR IN THOSE CASES

Most of the erroneous deductions which have sprung out of the indeterminateness conception appear to have arisen from the expansion to a generalization of the results of a particular isolated case. Mr. Flux, in reviewing Mr. J. A. Hobson's *Economics of Distribution*, based on ideas similar to those which we have just discussed, remarked: "That the gradations of any actual supply or demand schedule do not proceed by the infinitesimal changes assumed in the mathematical treatment of the problems of value may be granted. It need not follow that the gradations, though finite, are of a magnitude requiring as much attention as demanded in the book under discussion."[105] The important consideration, however, is not the size of units or gradations of supply and demand as affecting the size of transactions, but the influence of the time element, which causes the normal competitive economic forces to be effective.

JEVONS' TREATMENT IN "THE STATE IN RELATION TO LABOUR"

The treatment of bargains over large units was similar in Jevons' later work *The State in Relation to Labour* (1882), but he substituted for compara-

---

105. *Econ. Jour.*, 1900, p. 381.

tive "knowledge of each other's position and needs" the "combat of desires and fears," of the parties, a combat which, he thought, was "only solved by the lapse of time which tries the patience of both parties." In view of the apparent similarity of this position to that which exists in the case of a strike it seems desirable to examine the idea. In any *actual* case we should not find complete isolation, monopoly and uniqueness; and the term "combat" is not quite satisfactory. Both parties may be extremely keen to secure the exchange of the property on good terms; and if the sum of money involved is a large one, afraid of misjudging the value of the investment or realization. The reason why the would-be *seller* waits is so that he may test the market. The possible purchasers at any one moment of an indivisible property of large value may be very small, but there are potential purchasers who will, in course of time, come into the market. The seller's judgment of the probable extent of potential demand will determine the price he will be prepared to accept. His inclination will most likely be to agree to a lower price in the present than he believes he will probably be offered in the future because, in so doing, he will discount both time and risk. The reason why the *buyer* waits is that he believes there *is* no other buyer who is likely, within a reasonable space of time, to offer the price he is prepared to pay; or that by waiting he can find an equally good alternative at that price. As both are keen to make a transaction both are aware of some loss to themselves in delay. They will sooner or later be in a position to estimate whether their judgment was right or wrong and ultimately arrive at a price representing a rough coincidence of interest. Both parties may endeavor to "bluff"—that is, to create a false impression of the state of the market or their relationship to it—but the word "patience" explains nothing. If they had the means of forecasting the ultimate or long run demand or supply they would be relieved of the burden of waiting as a means of obtaining an indication of the position.

IN CHAPTER IV JEVONS HELD THAT TRADE UNIONS COULD NOT OBTAIN GENERAL AND PERMANENT INCREASES OF WAGES

Although obviously influenced by Thornton and Jenkin, Jevons did not indicate in his *Theory of Political Economy* that he thought the conception of indeterminateness was particularly applicable to the problem of labor's remuneration. That the idea may have been in his mind is suggested by the interpolation (almost as an afterthought) of the phrase: "It may be that indeterminate bargains of this kind" (e.g., over the sale of a house) "are best arranged by an arbitrator or third party"—an idea which is interesting in view of the later development of this idea by himself and others[106] in particular reference to labor. It was only after the appearance of *Mathematical Psychics*, however, that Jevons ventured to follow Edgeworth in arguing that the existence of combinations in trade disputes usually reduces them to a single contract bargain of the same indeterminate kind. He made the application to labor in his *State on Relation to Labour*, a treatise which appeared in April, 1882, a very short time after the publication of Edgeworth's book. The idea appears in the last chapter and seems rather in contradiction to the argument of the earlier chapters. There are, therefore, some grounds for a suspicion that it was hurriedly inserted. We certainly never get the impression from Jevons as from Edgeworth, that the creation or magnifying of such indeterminateness by combinations was "favourable to the unionists," or that owing to the neglect by economists of like considerations "the untutored mind of the workman had gone more straight to the point than economic intelligence."[107]

---

106. Especially by Prof. Pigou. "It is only because there is a margin of indeterminateness that the possibility and the need of (arbitration) exists" (*Principles and Methods of Industrial Peace*, p. 36).

107. *Mathematical Psychics*.

On the contrary, he had concluded "that it is quite impossible for trades unions in general to effect any permanent increase in wages,"[108] and that there were "two possible modes of increasing earnings: the one being to increase products, so as to have more to sell, and the second to decrease products in order to sell them at a higher price." Moreover, it followed "inevitably that if many or all people pursued the latter policy it would fail altogether"[109] "Obviously . . . ," he said, "the rate of wages which workmen can demand will depend upon the relation of supply to demand of such particular kind of labour."[110]

IN CHAPTER VII JEVONS REJECTED THE SUPPLY AND DEMAND THEORY OF WAGES AND BROUGHT IN "INDETERMINATENESS"

The remarkable thing is that the whole of the point of view here expressed, in fact, the complete argument of his Chapter IV, is, in Chapter VII on "Arbitration and Conciliation," casually superseded in a couple of pages (pp. 153-155) as being mere abstraction, an analysis of what would have been the case if things had been different from what, in reality, they were. "The existence, however, of combinations in the labour market," he wrote, "alters the nature of

---

108. Jevons, *The State in Relation to Labour*, 1882, p. 106.
109. *Ibid.*, p. 94.
110. *Ibid.*, p. 93.

the bargains altogether. The laws of supply and demand do not apply to such a case. In all bargains about a single object there may arise, as I have explained in my *Theory of Political Economy*, a deadlock." What he failed to show was that such examples could be linked in any useful way to the problem of bargains between combinations of capital and labor. Even if we could accept his assumption that they might be validly regarded as bargaining about a single object, there would still exist this radical difference, that whereas a contract over the sale of a house or an estate is a contract presumably for perpetuity, agreements between capital and labor are capable of being subjected to constant re-contract. But *can* bargains between combinations of capital and labor be legitimately regarded as concerned with anything resembling "a single object" or, as he had expressed it in his earlier book, "an indivisible object"? Surely, it is almost impossible to imagine anything more easily divisible than labor supplied. The two sides may haggle about the price per unit of labor but not about the amount of available labor that will be taken on at any given price. The price of labor will very rarely be immaterial to capitalists (even as perfect monopolists), in determining how much labor they can profitably employ, for instance. Each party may rely, however, on some immobility, temporary or permanent, of the factor of production owned by the other, causing a certain rigidity in the response of quantity to price; and Jevons might have extended his argument to cover this class of case. Instead, he introduced what seems at first a new consideration to explain indeterminateness—that is, the disutility of strikes and lock-outs to the parties.

POLITICAL ECONOMY IS NOT "SILENCED" UNDER BI-LATERAL MONOPOLY

"The men, for instance," he wrote, "ask for fifteen per cent advance of wages all round. Rather than have a strike, it might be for the interest of employers to give the advance or for the men to withdraw their demand; *a fortiori* any intermediate arrangement would still more meet their views." As in the case of the house transaction in his *Theory of Political Economy* he argued that there may be "absolutely no economic principle on which to decide the question." The disutilities of strikes and lock-outs can, of course, be paralleled with the loss from delay in that illustration, but a comparison is misleading. In the case of labor there is no inability to test the market through the absence of small increments; and the continuous refusal to contract in this case seems to be a delay with an entirely different motive. Even if we neglect "motives," we still cannot make a parallel, for in the former case the passage of time reveals the market or alternatives, whereas in the latter the very factors which normally reveal the market are suppressed. The object of the strike or lock-out when initiatory seems to be to obtain a price higher or lower than available alternatives to both parties would determine, and the power to do so ultimately rests upon control of alternatives—that is, upon the power to exploit monopoly. There are many elements of uncertainty in the determination of price in such circumstances. Apart from those which we have already noticed, the factors determining the extent of control or limitation in any case may be complex and uncertain, and hence the result unpredictable from this cause. The prices resulting may favor one party or the other, but there is no reason why we should say that economic principle fails to work; or as economists so careful as Sidgwick and, following him, Mr. L. L. Price, have held, that "where two combinations meet one another, political economy is perforce silenced."[111] Prof. Macgregor has pointed out in his *Industrial Combinations* that ". . . relative fewness tends to introduce elements which are more psy-

---

111. L. L. Price, *Economic Science and Practice*, p. 192. (Also in his *Industrial Peace*.)

chological than economic, though they can scarcely be called accidental to an economic analysis." [112] Judgment, of course, is less certain when transactions are few and potential demand and supply have to be estimated; and "bluff" may admittedly come in. These elements it seems are the only psychological ones which *mere fewness* necessarily brings in. Moreover, economic principle applies with equal relevance to conditions of relative monopoly as to conditions of relative competition. Not only is there no clear line of division between the two, but, to use Prof. Davenport's words, "It may indeed be said that in the main competitive and monopoly theory do not diverge, that the supply and demand analysis applies without change to monopoly and that monopoly differs from competition only in the fact that in monopoly the volume of supply is under centralised control, while in competition the limit of supply is found in marginal cost of production." [113]

MONOPOLIST CONTROL OF SUPPLY MAY BE DIRECT OR THROUGH PRICE CONTROL

Monopoly power rests ultimately upon the ability to limit or control supply. Such limitation or control may be direct—that is, scarcities may be created to

---

112. *Industrial Combinations,* pp. 69-70.
113. *Economics of Enterprise,* p. 482.

suit the interests of particular groups by direct restriction or exclusion (and much trade-union action is of this nature); or such limitation may be indirect —that is, monopolists may proceed by enforcing certain prices which suit them. It is combined resistance to attempts of the latter kind to enforce adverse prices that usually causes strikes or lock-outs to continue for more than one moment of time.

STRIKES AND LOCK-OUTS BEST REGARDED AS "COERCIVE DEVICES"

The problems we have just been considering are perhaps made clearer if we regard strikes and lock-outs (whether aggressive or defensive is immaterial) as *coercive devices*. Like a similar coercive weapon, "the boycott," they may be employed for a variety of motives and for the attainment of many different ends. They are a deliberate interference with the free and continuous flow of the services of the workers, capital equipment, or other factor of production in response to a given economic condition, competitive or monopolistic. Their object is generally either to force another party to acquiesce in a price other than the competitive or to resist such a price which another party seeks to impose. As we have already seen, the mere grouping in combinations of the owners of co-operant resources such as "property" and "labor" would not necessarily cause indeterminateness, provided transactions were made in small units. It is the joint determination by one group not to let another make contracts with individuals among them, which, judged by their available alternatives, would be most favorable to them, that creates the range of indeterminateness and the conditions in which a strike is possible; the determination that *all* transactions shall be made at a certain price (or more favorable ones) or there will be no transactions at all. For this reason we have additional grounds for saying that there is definitely a *"coercive"* element in such actions. The institution of property gives all monopolists the power to prevent access by other factors of production to the resources that they control. By that means the formation of a true socially determined price is prevented and a private coercion is substituted for a social coercion. (The meaning of "social coercion" is given below.) In the *absence* of monopoly, the institution of property may be held to be the very institution which causes the various factors of production to move to the most profitable channels as determined by society. In its *presence*, that view cannot be held.[114]

---

114. This must not, of course, be taken as implying a condemnation of "large" properties. In the community of the world a very

SUCCESSFUL STRIKES AND LOCK-OUTS ESTABLISH A
PRIVATE COERCION IN PLACE OF A SOCIAL COERCION

Where there is a complete absence of monopoly all individuals dealing in small increments are powerless in regard to price. They may give goods away, but we cannot call such happenings "transactions." Except in ignorance, or as a gift, or as a method of aggression to secure concessions, selling below or buying above the market price is inconceivable under perfect competition. Hence, when the market is the ruling force, we have what might be called "a social coercion," the impartial and impersonal ruling of society itself expressed in the resultant of those forces which make up the market. (The term "coercion" may seem the wrong word, for in this case it is definitely a product of the utmost freedom and mobility.) The monopolist aims at substituting for this socially determined price one that is believed to favor a particular group; and the power to do so is defi-

---

large property indeed may, through direct competition and that of substitutes and alternatives, be quite unable to exploit any monopoly power at all. But the usual defense of private property on economic grounds does not necessarily hold in such cases. That defense presupposes the most complete mobility and responsiveness of every unit of resources. It is only when this mobility and responsiveness exists that there can be any *certain* validity in what is thought to be a common assumption of economists that the price determined under private enterprise is the one which best serves the common good.

nitely obtained from a coercive power over individual cooperating units, preventing them from exercising that freedom which, under competition, results in the controlling power of market price.

THIS EXPLAINS THE "RANGE OF INDETERMINATENESS"

We can now come back to the idea of the range of indeterminateness. Is not the best explanation of it to be found in the fact that under bi-lateral monopoly you have two groups with coercive power of this kind, each attempting in the case of a strike to enforce a price against the interest of the other? The result may not be predictable, nor may the forces determining the ultimate price be expressible in schedules, but political economy is not "silenced." Quite apart from the economic nature of the coercive power, both parties will adjust their supply or demand according to the ruling price exactly as they would if the price had been fixed by the free market or legal enactment; and this remains the case as we shall see *although the actual division of the spoils of monopoly obtained at the expense of the consumer is largely an arbitrary affair;* and the limits to which either party will go will be influenced by the possibility of revision of the terms and other expected long-run reactions of their policy.

CAN MONOPOLY-GAINS BE MADE AT THE EXPENSE OF THE OWNERS OF OTHER FACTORS OF PRODUCTION?

Having considered the nature of the strike and monopoly coercion, we can now tackle the question of whether, by the exploitation of monopoly, the owners of one factor of production as a whole may gain at the expense of another—labor at the expense of the owners of property, for instance, or *vice versa*. (These groups are, of course, not naturally exclusive. Most property owners receive incomes from work and most "workers" own *some* property.)

PARTICULAR GROUPS MAY GAIN BY EXCLUDING OTHER FACTORS WHEN THEY ARE COMPETITIVE

Any *group* of persons together owning some portion of the factors of production may gain by keeping out of supply (or operation) certain factors of production owned by others; that is, they may gain as producers and sellers of certain commodities by preventing increments of factors owned by others, which might add to the supply of those commodities, from coming in to cooperate in the task of production. In so far as they can thus exclude, the total product (not necessarily its aggregate value) will be smaller. Thus their gain will be accompanied partly by loss to those excluded from cooperating in the task, and partly by loss to those who buy the commodity, who will have to pay a higher price per unit for the smaller quantity. What factors it will pay any particular group to exclude will depend upon several considerations. Other things being equal, it will certainly pay the workers in any particular case to exclude such factors as capital equipment or new methods of organization when they are "labor-saving," i.e. when their exclusion will mean that more workers can be employed at the same rate of wages or the same number at a higher rate of wages. In other cases, the exclusion of capital equipment, improved organization or other factors will result in a fall in demand for the workers themselves (although they might not realize this), and a gain to them is *not* certain. In regard to other supplies of like factors, however (workers of the same type, for example), exclusion will nearly always benefit the *particular group* practicing it: and the gain will have been at the expense of the owners of the units excluded, and accompanied by loss to the consumer and probably to other factors of production.

THE PHRASE "AT THE EXPENSE OF"

Before going further we need to devote some attention to the phrase "at the expense of." Any monopolist-gain by a single monopolist among co-operant producing groups is necessarily accompanied by loss to certain of the other groups, for one reason because at the higher price asked by the monopoly factor there is, even in the absence of direct exclusion, some fall in the number of units of it demanded, and a consequent fall in the number of units of work or service demanded from the factors of production which cooperate with it. Thus, a trade union exclusion of competing workmen from a particular job tends to make both the capitalist and the consumer worse off. We might therefore say that the trade union gains at the expense of excluded workers, capital and the consumer. Yet, in a discussion such as this, mainly concerned with the possibility of redistribution, it might be convenient to distinguish broadly between (1) the source of those gains to one party which are possible because of the nature or condition of a factor of production owned by some other party, that is, when it is "exploitable" or "excludable," and (2) those losses to owners of other factors which are incidental rather than direct, although not necessarily unimportant. For instance, there is usually no point in a labor monopoly excluding directly a body of non-competing but co-operant workers (i.e., those engaged on an entirely different, complementary process), for they will be worse off by so doing. But *any* exclusion which pays them may, incidentally, exclude *some* non-competing workers. We can distinguish here between the loss to those whom *it has paid* to exclude and the loss to those who also happen to be kept out by that policy. The gain may be said to be obtained by the exclusion of the former (although also accompanied by loss to the latter, but not by their exploitation, for it would be impossible to gain at their expense alone). And, again, monopoly profits which are obtainable by any factor solely because of inelasticity of demand for the commodity by the consumer, may be said to exploit him, although the other factors of production as a whole *may* be worse off as a result of the exploitation of that monopoly. Monopoly profits to a factor which are possible solely owing to immobility of other factors may be said to be obtained by exploiting them, although as a result of their exploitation the consumer is worse off. This use of the term "exploit" is purely for convenience; it makes no clear logical distinction,[115] and it is not implied that these "incidental losses" as we have called them are not highly important. Almost invariably monopoly-gains, no

---

115. The elasticity of supply of any "non-exploitable" co-operant factor in this sense will influence the degree to which it is desirable to exploit any other co-operant factor or the consumer.

matter to what factor, are accompanied by loss to the consumer.

A GROUP OF WORKERS MAY GAIN WITHOUT EXCLUSION AGAINST AN INELASTIC DEMAND

For the next stage of our argument it will be most useful to take first a particular case and ask: Is it possible for a group of workers to gain without exclusion of other workers? If so, by whose exploitation may we say they have gained? Let us assume first that all other factors are in competition among themselves. When the relationship of the workers to other factors of production and the demand for the commodity is such that the number of units of their labor demanded is inelastic to rises in their remuneration per unit (from whatever cause), the restriction of the amount offered by them at a price may mean a larger aggregate return to them. In other words, by forcing a price higher than the competitive, and practicing work-sharing or a restriction of output, every worker in the group may be better off than under competition, although no workers whom competitive remuneration would have attracted have been excluded. This appears to be what the Webbs mean when (in dealing with Edgeworth's contention on this point that combined parties tend to gain at the expense of uncombined parties with whom they are dealing) they say: "Nor need the combination amount in any sense to a monopoly." (*Industrial Democracy*, p. 653.) The action is, of course, essentially monopolistic, although not necessarily to be condemned on that account if it does result in a redistribution of the product of industry in favor of the relatively poor. "Because the total produce is diminished, it does not follow that the labourer's share is diminished (the loss may fall on the capitalist and entrepreneur whose compressibility has been well shown by Mr. Sidgwick)." (Edgeworth, *Mathematical Psychics*.)

IS RESTRICTION OF OUTPUT, THEN, TO THE INTERESTS OF THE WORKERS?

But does an examination of this hypothetical possibility enable us to say, as Edgeworth said in regard to the alleged disbelief of trade unionists in the wage-fund, that in the matter of the *work fund* "the untutored mind of the workman had gone more straight to the point than economic intelligence misled by a bad method, reasoning without mathematics upon mathematical subjects"? Does the road to plenty for the workers lie in restriction, work-sharing and "short time"?[116]

---

116. When a fund such as "unemployment donation" (provided by State or charity) exists to remunerate workers excluded, the whole body of workers may *conceivably* gain as a whole. But

GAINS OF THIS KIND RARE IN PRACTICE

Attempts to obtain pure gains of this nature seem to be very rare in practice. We find few cases of conscious and rational work-sharing. Trade-union officials think in terms of rates per head—not aggregates. There may, nevertheless, be some increment of this sort of gain combined with the gain from direct exclusion when unions are faced with an inelastic demand. If we allow for conditions which cause a certain inertia in the movement of economic factors, the conclusion suggests itself that inelastic demand for labor is ultimately very rare. The question of the demand for labor in general raises big difficulties which cannot be dealt with here. But from broad considerations of this kind we might, whilst frankly admitting the possibility of large gains to particular groups, deny the likelihood of any general improved redistribution between different factors of production or income classes. This would not satisfy the sceptic, however, and accordingly the following analysis is desirable.

---

this represents a direct transference of society's income which *could* have been effected equally well without trade union action, the resulting unemployment and its incidental loss.

WE CANNOT ASSUME ELASTICITY OF DEMAND FOR LABOR
WHERE OTHER FACTORS ARE CO-OPERANT AND NOT COMPETITIVE

To the extent to which a considerable part of the
other factors (e.g., capital equipment) can be "labor
saving," the condition of inelasticity is unlikely to
exist even in the short run, because of the possibility
of substitution. When, on the other hand, the marginal increments of other factors are co-operant rather
than competing in their relation to labor, we cannot
assume probable elasticity of demand.

THE POSSIBILITY OF ULTIMATE GAIN BY ARTIFICIAL WAGE
RATES DEPENDS UPON THE ELASTICITY OF DEMAND FOR
THE PRODUCT

When a group of workers raises the price per unit
of its work and adopts the device of work-sharing, the
effect is that in supplying less units for the process of
production they have allowed less units of the other
factors to cooperate; that is, they have excluded or
caused to remain idle that portion of those factors
which no longer finds its most profitable use in that
field. They must be able either to prevent such excluded units of other factors from cooperating with
other supplies of workers whom earnings above the
competitive level in the particular trade would tend
to attract, or to rely upon such cooperation being,
for other reasons, impossible. As we have assumed

that other factors are in competition the *ultimate* effect will be that increased costs will cause a diversion of the resources comprising those factors until the return to the marginal increment of each category thereof has fallen to normal. *When this has resulted*, it seems extremely improbable that the workers will have gained unless the demand for the commodity is inelastic. The elasticity of demand for the commodity will determine the price obtained by the competitive sellers for the smaller product, and hence the extent to which other resources will be driven away by the increased costs. A gain resulting from *this* circumstance, therefore, cannot be said to be obtained by exploiting property or any other factor, for only the nature of the demand for the product enables it to be realized. It is obtained by exploiting the consumer.

UNTIL CO-OPERANT FACTORS CAN MOVE THEY MAY BE EXPLOITED

Any monopoly increment accruing to the workers' group which does *not* result from this circumstance must arise from the fact that the diversion of other factors of production referred to above may be slow. Some resources we can conceive of as being transferred immediately there is any increase of costs, but there might be a long lag with others for which there are no sufficiently profitable alternative uses. The whole question turns principally on the elasticity of supply of other factors, which it is now convenient in view of current terminology to lump together under one heading as "capital." The supply of capital we must regard as being, *in the long run*, highly elastic. In respect of some forms of it, particularly new capital coming forward, it is obviously so; but in some other concerns, particularly those with large fixed plants, it seems at first sight to be the very reverse.

FACTORS MAKING FOR SHORT-RUN IMMOBILITY OF "CAPITAL"

In the short run, the elasticity of demand for labor of a particular concern is almost always inelastic. It may have, for instance, a contract to fulfill and be under a penalty for failure. In such circumstances a labor combination might demand and obtain a rise of fifty per cent in wages, and yet the numbers employed, even if the job had to be carried on at a loss, hardly fall off at all. It is perhaps in part owing to the ease with which gains may be made in this way at the expense of the *entrepreneur* that the terms of contracts often have a clause inserted to the effect that in the case of any changes in the remuneration of labor an adjusting modification of the price payable shall be made. There are many other kinds of short-run commitments the existence of which may make for temporary inelasticity of demand. Probably the most important of all is the necessity to pay interest on capital or on borrowed money where there are heavy overhead costs. Undertakings such as railways or other public works, in which capital consists largely in valuable plant and equipment that cannot be turned to other uses, are the outstanding example of this. At first, it seems that we have here a case in which labor can exploit capital, if not permanently, at least over a long period; and where demand is not expanding, capital *does* appear to be definitely exploitable. Yet, even in the extreme case of absolute immobility of capital, we can conceive of factors likely to cause some degree of elasticity. Quite apart from the possible substitution of labor-saving equipment new means of economizing labor are almost certain to become profitable when it is more expensive.

APPARENT EXPLOITABILITY OF IMMOBILE FACTORS MAY PROVE ILLUSORY

In practice, for many reasons, when considerable rises in general costs cannot be passed on to the consumer, *some* part of the total capital equipment will be closed down. There will most likely be a hard struggle before such action is considered, but as soon as it becomes clear that absolute loss cannot be avoided on the operation of a particular section of plant, then it will be laid idle. In such a case a new equilibrium will be *suddenly* realized after a time, and at a single moment a large number of workers may be at once dismissed. How soon such a result will follow any increase of costs will depend upon how near the unprofitable point the unit of plant involved happens to be before that increase. This suggests that in practice such elasticity of demand for labor as there is, is effective, so to speak, "in jerks." Increased wages which occasion little reduction in numbers employed might, if raised a little further, result in a considerable reduction. Hence, whereas it is theoretically possible, from the factors we have so far considered that, in particular cases, labor stands to gain, it must be remembered that whether the necessary theoretical conditions will be present or not in any case will be in some degree a matter of chance. Unless the true position is realized adequately in each case a rise in wages may often result in a large drop in numbers employed.

WHEN SUCH POLICIES BECOME NORMAL, NO CO-OPERANT FACTOR IS EXPLOITABLE

But however strong the probability that capital will be exploitable in such circumstances, we cannot validly generalize from the particular. If it were really normal for labor to exploit capital invested in this class of undertaking, the result would be that less would be invested in this class. Owing to the risk of such exploitation capital would be diverted to channels which, through that risk, would become relatively profitable. New capital is absolutely mobile. Or, to put the matter in more general terms, resources are attracted to particular productive channels in the light of the claims on the value of the product made by co-operant factors. Where competition exists there is no expectation that the size of other claims will be permanent except for the contract period; but resources will only be directed into channels in which they must become immobile in the light of the probable future variation through competition of the terms demanded by the others. Where artificial interferences through monopoly or State regulations are general it is in the light of the expected course of *their* results that resources will be attracted. Thus, once collective bargaining or legal enactment becomes the normal policy, no co-operant factor of producion is in itself exploitable.

THE SIZE OF THE UNIT OF SUPPLY IS IRRELEVANT

The size of the technical unit of supply makes no difference to this principle at all. The supply of plant that is only possible in large units reacts to intensification of demand in exactly the same way as does plant for industries of different form, except that it does so "in jerks." Thus, although a particular increase in wages costs may not result in a large falling off in numbers employed ~~it may have prevented a large falling off in numbers employed~~ it may have prevented a large increase which was imminent. In practice, these considerations are somewhat masked by the fact that such concerns are themselves in some degree monopolistic and can withstand increased costs up to a point by placing a further burden on the consumer.

EXPLOITATION OF "CAPITAL" A BREACH OF FAITH WITH INVESTORS IN IMMOBILE RESOURCES

The exploitation of capital by particular groups of workers is, thus, impossible except during the first transition from competition to monopoly or regulation; and such exploitation might be regarded as a breach of faith on the part of Society with those who have chosen to invest in relatively immobile resources. We must, however, bear in mind that the probability of aggregate gain is, even in this class of case, not high. (As we have seen above.)

"LABOR" NO MORE EXPLOITABLE THROUGH IMMOBILITY THAN "CAPITAL"

In the same way, the general exploitation of "labor" by "capital" through its immobility can be shown to be equally impossible. Once again, the question can be approached by considering elasticity of supply, which is probably greatest among laborers, the completely unspecialized class. Workers of this kind, although their territorial mobility may be small (in so far as they correspond to the most poorly paid class), have yet a wide range of alternative occupations. The chief restrictions on their mobility are those which have been created by labor organizations themselves and are clearly against the advantage of owners of capital generally. Here also, as with the supply of capital, in the very short run the supply of labor is inelastic and capable, in particular cases and during the first transition from competition to monopoly among capitalists, of temporary exploitation. But with the progress of modern industrial organization and technique and the growing tendency for labor to lose its specialization, as skill is thrown more and more on to the machine, the power even in these circumstances to obtain short-run gains through immobility becomes less and less possible. In practice, for many reasons, reductions of wages sought for by capitalists involve relatively small percentages except in times of monetary disturbance when prices generally are fluctuating rapidly. Undue lowering of wages can be met by a gradual migration of the more efficient workers to the considerable disadvantage of the injudicious firm. There is no parallel in labor to the immobility of huge capital units.

DELIBERATELY IMPOSED RESTRICTIONS ON MOBILITY OF LABOR NOT ADVANTAGEOUS TO CAPITAL IN GENERAL

The principle remains the same even if, for the sake of argument, we suppose it to be possible for the capitalist to impose deliberate restrictions on the mobility of labor. In so far as a capitalist can, by any device, prevent his workers from moving to take advantage of the labor market elsewhere he can, it seems, obviously gain at their expense. The more effective his power, it appears, the greater will be his gain. Surely, it will be said, laws or institutions designed to keep agricultural workers on the land, for instance, will benefit the farming community in so far as they succeed. The answer is that more of the other resources of the country will remain in or flow into that form of enterprise. In cases where such restrictions have been imposed under changing conditions, and until a new equilibrium has been reached, and so long as competition from existing or potential farmers can be prevented, the profitableness of farming will be above the normal. But it hardly seems likely that suppression of competition would be possible in the case of so large a group, even for a short time. In any case it does not follow from this that labor in general will lose relatively to capital in general, even in the short run (including all other factors of production under the heading "capital"). For labor elsewhere will probably benefit through the relative scarcity of labor, and capitalists elsewhere lose through that same scarcity. Further analysis of this *unimportant* point would have to consider the effect of relative elasticities of demand for the different factors in competitive and non-competitive channels. But this is a question on which we can formulate so few valid generalizations that it seems desirable to regard it as a chance consideration affecting the result.

NEW LABOR COMING FORWARD UNEXPLOITABLE
EVEN IN THE SHORT RUN

The same reasoning applies in regard to incidental immobility, i.e. that which is not the result of deliberate contrivance. Where there has been temporary exploitation of an immobile labor group, workers in other groups will tend to lose, not to gain, as it is overcome; and capitalists elsewhere will tend to gain as labor becomes more plentiful to them. Trade-union demarcations and artificial restriction on entrance to different occupations, State regulation of wages, and generally policies which hinder labor transference— all tend to create the conditions in which exploitation of the kind we are considering may appear to be possible in particular cases. It seems that if a large number of occupations have their entrance restricted, openings for adequate alternative employment for those workers who feel themselves to be unfairly treated will be so limited that they will have to lower their supply price considerably in order to get absorbed. Such short-run monopoly-gains as *are* possible to capitalists through the existence of such conditions must, of course, be offset by the monopoly-gains of those groups of workers whose protective system alone enables the capitalist to exploit. But in regard to the constant flow of new labor coming

forward, however irrational we may believe the choice
of trades to be, we may yet presume that trades whose
workers are being "exploited" by employers owing
to their acquired or incidental immobility will be
avoided.

THE CONSUMER ALONE IS ULTIMATELY EXPLOITABLE BY COLLECTIVE ACTION

To sum up our main conclusions so far: we have
seen that combined labor cannot be said to exploit
the co-operant factors of production possessed by
the capitalist, and that labor combinations do not
enable workers in general to exploit capital in general. The ultimate gains of workers by combination
when not at the expense of excluded competitors
are obtained by exploiting the consumer; for the
extent to which capital will be excluded by decreased supply of labor at a higher cost per unit
will depend upon elasticity of demand for the *commodity*, which will determine the margin which
gives the normal rate of return. We have also seen
that combined capital not practicing exclusion of
those whom *competitive* profits would attract cannot be said to gain by exploiting the worker but by
exploiting the consumer. Briefly, the import of these
conclusions may be summarized as follows:

No factor of production can maintain the co-operation of another factor by offering it or leaving it an amount of the product less than the value of its net product elsewhere. The extent to which demand for the product falls off as its price is raised determines the quantity of one factor that will be driven away by another factor getting a larger share. Hence, we can say that monopoly-gains by any factor are ultimately obtained by exploiting the consumer, although incidental losses are usually thrown upon other co-operant factors.

WHY THE ERRONEOUS BELIEF HAS ARISEN

The widespread belief that monopoly-gains (or gains by wage regulation) are obtainable by labor and capital at one another's expense seems to have arisen (1) from the belief that if any or all wage rates are raised artificially, workers as a whole will get more; and (2) from the habit of regarding "labor" and "capital" as in opposition rather than as co-operators in production.[117]

---

117. In so far as they are *competitors* they may gain at one another's expense by excluding units of competing resources, e.g. successful labor opposition to labor-saving machinery, etc. It is not suggested that such a policy can be to the *general* advantage of either party. The reverse can be shown.

LOWER WAGE RATES
MAY MEAN HIGHER AGGREGATE EARNINGS

The popular view ignores completely the possibility that the aggregate amount paid in wages might be increased by a shifting (directly or through recruitment) of workers from lower-paid to higher-paid jobs, even if there were many substantial reductions in wage *rates* and (what would be unlikely to happen in practice) there was no corresponding rise in the less well-paid jobs. Still less does the popular view take account of the increase in the aggregate welfare of the workers which would result from greater equality caused by such a redistribution.

AS THE CONSUMER IS ALONE EXPLOITABLE WE EXPECT
TO FIND AND DO FIND "JOINT MONOPOLIES"

The habit of regarding labor and capital as in opposition has been encouraged by economic text-books. It may be convenient for some purposes to represent their relations to one another by supply and demand schedules, so long as it is not forgotten that the ultimate demand for both of them is the demand for their jointly produced product. As monopoly gains, both to workers' and to capitalists' combinations, are ultimately obtained solely by limiting the supply of the commodities, it is not surprising that we find joint monopolies, that is, different co-operant factors of production consciously or tacitly practicing monopoly together and dividing the spoils. A joint monopoly is a greatly strengthened one, and represents a concentration of interests against those excluded. It is a particular case of vertical combination (generally tacit). Often, it will definitely pay an employers' monopoly that its employees shall combine. If there is any body of workers free to cooperate with a rival manufacturer whom monopoly prices would bring into the field the capitalist's monopoly is threatened; and this accounts for the frequent agreement between an employers' combination and a trade union for the payment of a high wage provided that the union will see that no workers at all in that occupation shall be employed at less. In modern times the State has intervened to strengthen such joint monopolies, either by making agreements arrived at by industrial councils binding on the trade or by direct legal enactment. Combined workers themselves have nearly always encouraged their employers to combine also. They have been strong advocates of price agreements, have roundly condemned "cut-throat" competition, and have asked for State help to protect "the good employer." In joint monopoly is to be found the explanation of most trade-union action in these times, and of much capital combination at all times.

THE INDETERMINATENESS OF "THE QUOTA"

There is always an arbitrary element in the division of monopoly spoils. In the case of the quota system with a capital monopoly, or a system of work-sharing by a trade union, the problem is always there of deciding how many shall be allowed to participate at all. In the case of a trade union it will probably be the normal number employed before the exercise or further exercise of monopoly power. And then we get the problem of how *different kinds* of participants shall share in the proceeds. In the case of a group of workers engaged on the same process "the standard rate" usually settles the matter, although there may still be some grading according to ability. When we get two groups of workers sharing the monopoly but engaged on non-competing or complementary (co-operant) processes, some formula roughly based on "justice" may be applied; e.g. we may get the proceeds divided more or less in proportion to former competitive earnings, or supposed difficulty of the task or technical status, etc. There is, however, no certain exterior principle such as the market to refer to in this division: from some points of view it is a purely arbitrary affair. In regard to considerations which can be usefully expressed or represented in schedules or curves, the division among them is "indeterminate." As a rule, equal division per head of workers seems to be sufficiently just: they are seldom conscious of any serious divergence of interest between different groups. Yet, in essence, the problem of the division between workers of the monopoly increment is the same as in the case of joint monopoly between capital and labor.

THE ADVANTAGE IN COLLUSION

Now joint monopolists may either act independently, or in collusion (deliberate or tacit). If they act independently and seek to maximize their own share of the monopoly-gain, the aggregate gain will be, other things being equal, smaller than if they act in collusion. For in acting independently they will each restrict their contribution in response to the terms on which they can get the other factors to cooperate. If any one factor only is a monopolist, it will presumably so limit its contribution as to maximize the return to it, given what competition commands shall be paid to the other factors. Any increase in costs to that monopolized factor (whether due to monopoly of another factor or not is immaterial) will presumably cause it to reduce its contribution still further in order to maximize, not the aggregate received for the commodity, but its share of the total. As it is to the obvious advantage of all factors considered together that the greatest aggregate shall be obtained, we can say that each monopolist factor seeking its own end does not serve their general good. No matter what division of the proceeds finally results (within the range of indeterminateness), collusion in regard to output will benefit all factors, for no factor need get less and all may get more than under independent action. Hence, we may expect to find, and in practice we do find, some measure of tacit collusion, or forebearance and "reasonableness" among co-operant monopolistic groups.

JOINT MONOPOLY IN THE EARLY NINETEENTH CENTURY

It is impossible in this essay adequately to indicate the significance in economic history of joint monopoly of this kind. All that can be done is to suggest grounds for the belief that its importance has been greatly under-estimated. It has already been pointed out that practically all the combinations among employers that were revealed by the inquiries in England in 1824 and 1825 were either retaliatory against unions exploiting "the strike in detail" or else the employers' side of joint monopolies operating with the encouragement and connivance of the workers. Francis Place merely wanted the Combination Laws repealed, and had no interest in bringing out the true significance of the evidence which was brought forward. His comment on an obvious case of joint monopoly was: "Employers advised the men to combine. Thus it appears the law is so iniquitous that those in whose favour it was made encourage the men to break it." (Note written on his copy of the Report of the 1824 *Select Committee on Artisans and Machinery*, p. 279). Even in the days when combinations were illegal there is much evidence of employers encouraging their men to combine. There seems to have been a good deal of it among the Framework Knitters, directly fostered by the masters.[118] And we find just as frequently cases of organized workmen petitioning their employers and urging them to combine: the Journeymen Coach-Makers were trying during 1816 and 1817 to get their masters to organize.[119] The rules of the Journeyman Paper-Makers of 1823 included a doggerel verse beginning with the ominous words: "May masters

---

118. E.g., Evidence of Thorpe and Ben Taylor. *Report of Select Committee on Artisans and Machinery*, 1824, pp. 274, 281.

119. Place Add. MSS. 27799:147-8.

with their men unite."[120] Other cases of joint monopoly (or attempts to protect the "honourable masters" as they were called), before 1824 were found among the Rochdale weavers,[121] the Stockport Cotton Spinners, the Dublin Saddlers, the Hosiers, the Shipwrights, the Calico Printers, and many other established trades of that day.[122] It was always the "honourable employers" whom they sought to protect; and the same phraseology remains today. In those early times they had even conceived of the utility of the device known today as "extension of agreements" which is found in conjunction with legislation concerning industrial councils and arbitration courts in so many parts of the world. In 1824 the Lace-Makers petitioned Sir J. Hobhouse to introduce a bill "for regulating wages by the decisions of a board composed of selected masters and men, and making the scale thus agreed upon binding on the trade. . . ."[123] He refused.

---

120. *Report of Select Committee on Combination Laws*, 1825, p. 59.

121. *Ibid.*, p. 154.

122. The Reports of the Committees of 1824 and 1825 already referred to are full of evidence, direct and indirect on this point, as are also the Place MSS. and cuttings. We find the same phenomenon during the seventeenth and eighteenth centuries.

123. Felkin, *History of the Machine Wrought Hosiery . . .* etc., p. 344.

INADEQUATE RECOGNITION OF THE SIGNIFICANCE OF
"JOINT MONOPOLY"

The nineteenth century is full of further examples
of joint monopoly. Yet, as already pointed out, it
has received singularly little recognition except by
casual comment of unimportant writers. A pamphlet
in 1867 recognized that "the means which secure the
workmen the monopoly of labour, secure the masters
also from any heavy pressure of competition."[124] In
1905, a writer on *Employers' Associations* recognized
that they were "but a logical step in, and the natural
complement of, the trade-union movement," and that
they were "an essential feature (of it) without which
it would be impossible for it to accomplish the purposes for which it exists."[125] But we seldom find so
certain an understanding of this relation between
employers' and workers' combinations. This is perhaps because *formal* combinations between capital
and labor have been rare. In the late 'nineties of last
century a number of open alliances of this kind were
flourishing in England in certain hardware, furniture
and china trades. The leading advocate of this form
of organization was one E. J. Smith, who had no very
clear idea of the economic implications of the de-

---

124. H. M. White, *The Principles of Trade Unionism*, 1867, p.
17.

125. *Quarterly Journal of Economics*, 1905, p. 110.

velopments he advised. His schemes received the cordial approval of the *Economic Review* and were by no means regarded as against the general interest by the *Economic Journal*.[126] The injurious and monopolistic nature of such organizations was, however, pointed out by Prof. Cannan[127] and by Prof. Pigou.[128] About the same time similar organizations had grown up on the Continent—"Les Syndicats Mixtes" of France. None of these alliances resulted in very close bodies and they do not appear to have survived for long.

IMPORTANCE OF JOINT MONOPOLY IN MODERN SOCIETY

If open and deliberate alliances like these have been rare, cases of tacit mutual support of each other by capitalist and labor groups have been widespread, and are typical of modern economic society. They have been encouraged and developed by tariff and industrial legislation—especially by arbitration, conciliation, and wage regulation acts. In joint monopoly, the writer believes, we have the real clue to the understanding of "anti-sweating" movements, which have not yet, in his opinion, received adequate impartial

126. See paragraph, obviously written by Edgeworth, in *Econ. Jour.*, 1898, p. 227.

127. *Econ. Jour.*, 1900, p. 63.

128. *Principles and Methods of Industrial Peace.*

study. In the present stage of development, when the size of the monopoly unit is tending to become larger, and when capitalist monopoly tendencies are made respectable by the adoption of the propagandist euphemism "rationalization,"[129] the same relationship is there on a larger scale. Dr. Robert Liefmann's proposal that trade-union representatives should be admitted to cartel directorates and that employers should have permanent representatives on trade-union executives is a good manifestation of it.

OUR ASSUMPTION HERE OF RATIONAL ACTION BY MONOPOLISTS NOT JUSTIFIABLE IN PRACTICE

The practical results of the widespread existence of collective bargaining may be more harmful than this discussion has suggested. For convenience and simplicity we have made here certain assumptions in regard to rational action on the part of combinations which cannot be justified in practice. The truth is that only the vaguest guesses as to the long-run elasticity of demand for products are possible in the actual economic world; and we find, as a result, that bilateral monopoly creates "indeterminateness" of

---

129. It is deplorable that this term has become so closely associated in the Press with quota schemes and price-fixing cartels. Unfortunately, the stress is nearly always on "ration" not "rational."

wage rates in another sense—through causing the price and wage-fixing mechanism to lose its sensitiveness. There arises a process of higgling between large and clumsy units in which the forces determining the settlement have only a remote connection with the interests of those members of the community who will be affected by the result. So undefinable are the forces which in such circumstances actually bring about the result that the adjective "indeterminate" well fits the case. Within the complex of factors determining price there are none which are sufficiently constant to be honored with the name of "cause." It often appears to the writer that the continued appearance of industrial depression in Great Britain is primarily due to the widespread existence of monopolistic bodies on both sides which (quite apart from their having caused equipment and labor to remain idle by policies aiming at "not spoiling the market") have destroyed the sensitiveness of the price and particularly the wage system.

EXPLOITATION OF THE CONSUMER HITS THE WORKING-CLASS MOST HEAVILY

The above analysis has sought to show that the ultimate gains of trade unions as well as monopolies of capital are obtained either by the "exploitation" of the consumer or the exclusion of competitors (although in the latter case, of course, the consumer also loses). In regard to gains at the consumers' expense, the effect upon distribution will depend upon the extent to which the owners of different factors of production are the final consumers of the product concerned. In fact, we find that the greater part of the demand for consumers' goods is exercised by relatively poor people, and most of the commodities in whose manufacture the working-class are employed are consumed by themselves as a class. This is a question of fact which has often been commented on.[130] Hence, apparent gains by workers at the expense of the consumer are likely, in general, to cause a more than proportionate real loss to them. If trade unions had, and exercised, the power to break down capitalists' monopolies they would benefit the workers of the community as consumers, but in practice their effect is to bolster up the capitalist's exclusiveness and to erect a dyke (against potential competition) covering an even larger area.

TRADE UNIONS ARE THE WRONG INSTITUTION FOR ATTEMPTING TO IMPROVE DISTRIBUTION

Workers' combinations are impotent to secure a redistribution of the product of industry in favor of

---

130. E.g., cf. Pigou, *Economics of Welfare,* Second Edn., pp. 646-8,

the relatively poor. Such a result cannot be achieved by interference with the value mechanism. Economists are all clearly conscious of the desirability of a more equal distribution of wealth; indeed, they base their case for it upon the firm foundation that it will lead to a maximization of economic welfare, and not upon abstractions such as "natural right" or "justice." There are means of achieving greater equality that will still allow the value mechanism to function freely. It can be achieved by the thoughtful modification of economic institutions. But the consideration of this point lies outside the scope of this essay.

THE "LEGITIMATE" FUNCTIONS OF TRADE UNIONISM ARE PERHAPS CONCERNED WITH OTHER MATTERS THAN WAGE RATES

The rate of wages which is best for the workers as a whole is that which is determined in the free market. The main useful function of collective bargaining may perhaps be negotiating about those things which, unlike prices or rates of wages, are *not* adequately determined by the market process. For example, hours of work and conditions of work are things that intimately concern workmen and are best decided collectively. They are a social matter, and ought, if possible, to express the will of the majority. "The *employer*" is concerned not so much with wages, hours, or conditions of work as with labor costs. Once it is recognized that shorter hours, or extra workshop comforts that cost money and do not add to efficiency, tend, in the absence of monopoly, to reduce wages, collective bargaining becomes an excellent thing. So long as one of the factors making up total labor costs is allowed to vary in harmony with economic change the value mechanism in society can continue to work. One cost factor at least must be a variable, and it is desirable that it should be the one which is most sensitive to change and therefore the most reliable index to guide human effort. That condition is satisfied by the rate of wages.

NOTE.—Since the final proofs of this book were returned the author has seen the manuscript of an acute and lucid article by Mr. J. R. Hicks which criticizes the contributions of Edgeworth and Marshall to the theory of wage indeterminateness. The article will, it is understood, shortly appear in the *Economic Journal*. It gives strong general support to the main thesis of this book, and in particular fills the gap left by the omission here of the detail of Edgeworth's discussion.

Index

Date Due

JUL 27 '76			
PRINTED	IN U. S. A.